Wow, I don't know if I agree with half this book, but it's a fun read.
Enjoy!

"Big Sis"

unleashing
the
sex goddess
in
every
woman

Also by Olivia St. Claire

203 WAYS TO DRIVE
A MAN WILD IN BED

unleashing

the

sex goddess

in

every

woman

bantam books

olivia st. claire

ISBN 0 7338 0003 3.

First published in Australia and New Zealand
in 1996 by Bantam, a division of
Transworld Publishers (Aust) Pty Limited,
15–25 Helles Ave, Moorebank, NSW 2170,
and Transworld Publishers (NZ) Limited,
3 William Pickering Drive, Albany, Auckland.

Published by arrangement with Harmony Books, a
division of Crown Publishers, Inc., 201 East 50th
Street, New York, New York 10022.

Printed in the United States of America
Design by John Fontana with Linda Kocur

To the sensual goddesses of history and heaven—especially

Aphrodite, Cleopatra, the Cloud Damsels, the Cosmic Yoni, the

Djanggawo sisters, Hathor, Inanna, Lilith, Mother Earth,

Nofretari, Oshun, Pele, Sekhmet, Shakti, the Snake Priestess,

White Buffalo Woman, Wild Woman, Xochiquetzal, the

Yoginis—and to the Sex Goddess in every woman

Acknowledgments

My deepest gratitude to all the women and men who so graciously shared their most intimate thoughts and feelings with me—we have all learned so much from you. Heartfelt thanks as well to the extraordinary women who so lavishly gave me their support, advice, assistance, and love during the writing of this book—Christine, Claudia, Deborah, Jane, Karen Marie, Marianne, Pamela, Paula, Sandy, and Tovi; to those who have so expertly guided me in birthing it into the world—Shaye, Paula, Shima, and Miko; and most especially to Henri, my wild inspiration, who has a magical knack for unearthing the most deeply hidden caves of my Inner Sex Goddess.

Contents

unleashing

the

sex goddess

in

every

woman

bantam books

olivia st. claire

A woman learns to be a
good lover from her own
heart and from the heart
of her being. She does not
need to learn it from a
man. She learns it from
her inner goddess.
—Elaine Kittredge,
<u>Masterpiece</u>
<u>Sex</u>

1

awakening

your

inner

sex goddess

every woman has an Inner Sex Goddess. She lives in your heart, your body, and your senses. She is the part of you that feels aroused by reading erotic literature or watching sexy movies. She is the part of you that skips a heartbeat when an attractive man in tight jeans walks by. She is the part of you that feels coy and flirtatious when you put on a clingy dress; after all, it was *her* idea to wear the dress in the first place. Your Inner Sex Goddess is the one who bought this book and who tingles with anticipation at the thought of becoming, at last, her most gloriously seductive self.

Whether you experience her as a feeling (like a buttery inner warmth), as one of the many roles you play in life (such as career woman, mother, friend, wife, party organizer), or as a distinct personality (like your inner child, inner critic, or inner male and female), your Inner Sex Goddess is a strong, important, and natural part of who you really are. And getting to know her is really getting to know your deepest self—your beliefs and values, your fears and dreams, and the very personal poetry of your body. The truly wonderful thing about your Inner Sex Goddess is that, without instruction from any person, book, workshop, or man, she already knows how to be fabulously sexy and alluring. In her bones, she knows how to *feel* sexy, even when you're tired and cranky, bored, or simply at a loss for inspiration. She knows exactly what to do with her hands when you are making love; she doesn't wonder if it's better to stroke his back or tickle his ear because, with unerring instinct, she automatically does the very thing that will most stimulate herself and her lover.

In fact, your Inner Sex Goddess is a boundless source of sexual energy, know-how, and charisma. Unashamed, self-confident, and regally proud of her sexuality, she understands that feeling and being sexy is a natural and beautiful way for a woman to nourish her spirit and learn to love the ecstasies of her sensation-rich body. Revealing herself to you with every swish of your hair or sway of your hip, your Inner Sex Goddess revels in the textures of life and the world of the senses—and the more you revel in those textures and senses, the better you will get to know her; the freer she will be to enjoy pleasuring herself and her lover; and the more lovely, bold, and exciting she will become.

It is she who lives in the vivid sensitivities of your body. She is there when you appreciate the look of candlelight on the curve of your breast, the smell of a gardenia in your hair, the taste of wine on your lips and tongue, the feel of sun or silk on your skin, the sound of sultry jazz or samba music, the luxury of a hot bubble bath or a full-body massage, the delicious flushes and tingles of self-pleasuring or lovemaking. These physical sensations are doorways to your rich inner world of lush romance and hot libido.

In fact, we women have a natural gift for combining romance, love, and sex into one magical art form. Even our enticingly soft and curvy bodies seem to be specially designed for exquisite pleasure. Did you know, for instance, that we females are unique in having a highly sensitive organ whose *only* purpose is sexual delight?

But even though we have all these natural erotic gifts, no one has schooled us in the art of being in tune with and expressing our inherent sexuality. So we have felt awkward, confused, and even cut off from one of the most precious and vital parts of ourselves. This is not the case in many indigenous cultures — for instance, Native American, tribal African, Tantric Indian, and some ancient Far Eastern societies, to name a few. Placing a high priority on developing sexual joy and proficiency in a sacred, loving way, these traditions often use specially trained sexual mentors to instruct and advise young people on how to appreciate the beauty and majesty of their bodies, as well as how to bring the highest sensual pleasure to their future partners — and to themselves. Naturally in touch with their Inner Sex Gods and Goddesses, people in these cultures believe sexuality is a divine gift and learn to treat their bodies with the utmost respect and reverence. We would be wise to learn from them.

the natural textures of life

Ancient indigenous cultures who were living closer to the earth and practicing rituals tied to the cycles of nature were more in tune with the senses and textures of life than our modern "civilized" society. Their uncomplicated existence and natural belief in the divine nature of plants, animals, elements, and life itself allowed them to be more intimately acquainted with the sensuality that dwelt within them—and left them with practically no inhibitions. To them, sexuality was a natural part of creation, and their sex organs were a chalice of the sacred energy of life. For example, one Stone Age cave painting shows a male figure holding a bow, his penis connected by an unbroken "power line" to the genitals of a female figure, suggesting that the female ritually empowered the man to go out for the hunt—archetypal roles that these early peoples acted out in daily life. In ancient India, men and women transformed themselves into gods and goddesses—meditating, anointing themselves, drinking sacred potions, muttering mantras over their bodies, and having ritualized sex—for the purpose of achieving enlightenment. Other pre-patriarchal religions honored fertility, creation, and sexuality in their ceremonies as different aspects of the same divine force. The pagan rites of Beltane, for example, involved ritual or wildly abandoned sexual activity as the symbolic cause of the earth's fertility in spring, and the solstice celebrations of planting and reaping the crops as a gift from the sensual, abundant body of the earth as goddess.

The women of all these cultures innately understood that the power and divine sexuality of the feminine principle was inherent not only in the earth, the elements, the animals, and the goddesses their people worshiped but also in their own sex organs and instincts, in the smells and tastes of their fleshy bodies, and in the natural textures of their lives. They and their individual Inner Sex Goddesses lived interchangeably with each other on a daily basis, moving smoothly and powerfully from conjugal bed to cooking fire to sexual fertility rite to tribal council to wheat harvest to sacramental childbirth and back again. Though we have centuries of acculturation and stifling moral convention to conquer, we too can become the natural sex goddesses these women were born and raised to be. When we come to know, revere, and love our bodies and their pleasures, as they did, we will no longer see our sexuality as something separate from our everyday selves. For with knowledge, reverence, and love come power, respect, responsibility, control—and the natural manifestation of each woman's own brand of lusty and graceful sexual divinity.

Finding your particular version of vampiness means exploring the hitherto unknown territories of your body, your senses, and your hot-blooded imagination. Your Inner Sex Goddess waits there in the intoxicating realm of self-knowledge and self-pleasuring. In our quest to know her, then, we'll be investigating many of the different avenues of pleasure through which you may find and unleash her, including:

- Transforming reading, writing, breathing, walking to work, and wearing clothes into aphrodisiacs for your senses
- Reveling in creative autoeroticism and self-pleasuring
- Having revealing inner dialogues with your goddess self
- Exploring and eroticizing every square inch of your body
- Inventing and enjoying wanton fantasies, dreams, and visions
- Discovering new G-spots and lovemaking talents
- Having lots of earthshaking orgasms
- Playing with erotic toys, clothes, and props
- Making wild passionate love to your man

But before we venture onto the superhighway of rich physical sensation, let's start by exploring some simple but very fruitful *mental* pathways to your sensual kingdom. Your sexuality is contained not only in your five physical senses but also in the inner senses of your mind and heart, and the journey to your Inner Sex Goddess begins not with your lover or some esoteric technique but within the private realm of your fantasies, heartfelt desires, daydreams, and self-created images about who you are. Experiment with the following ideas and see which ones resonate for you.

daily dialog

Throughout the day make a habit of asking your Inner Sex Goddess how she would do things. Just pretend that there is some creature inside you who knows how to be appropriately and naturally sexy, and have a conversation with her. Ask her, "How would you dress this morning? walk down the street? talk to that man? move your hips? dance? put on your makeup? wear your hair? How would you make yourself *feel* sexy? In what ways would you pleasure yourself? What toys would you use? How would you respond? Which man would you choose? How would you make love to him? Where would you put your hand?" Maybe she would add a silk scarf to the conservative outfit you put on. Maybe she would walk to work through the sensation-stimulating park rather than taking the boring bus. Perhaps she would tango in the kitchen instead of going to the gym. Follow her advice and see where it takes you.

journal

Start keeping a journal for your Inner Sex Goddess. Slip into her mind and heart and jot down what you see through her eyes, hear through her ears, feel through her emotions, think through her thoughts, and do through her body. Let her write about what she'd like to do, how she'd like you to relate to her, how she feels about herself, and how she'd like to express herself. Ask her questions about your sexuality and let her write the answers for you.

When I did this one time, my Inner Sex Goddess wrote down that if you view any sensual act not as something you do but as something you receive, as she does, it takes on a whole new meaning. For instance, when you kiss your lover, don't think of what you are doing to him with your lips, but instead focus on receiving the softness of *his* lips, receiving the smooth texture of the skin on his neck, receiving the hard round energy of his fingers as you suck on them. She said to close your eyes and concentrate on drinking in your lover's very essence. As much as I have attuned myself to the many nuances of lovemaking, I never would have thought about kissing quite this way. But keeping a journal for my Inner Sex Goddess brought out a wonderful new perspective that I have since eagerly incorporated into my love life. Find out what unique insights await you when you visit with your inner sexual divinity.

bodyknowing

A particularly sensual woman I know says, "For me, being in touch with my sexuality means deliberately cultivating a sort of magnetic, earthy feeling. I focus on being fully in my body and using all of its instincts and sensations, really feeling the electromagnetic energy pulsing around me. I imagine that I am a wild creature of the earth, a wolf woman, and knower of the moon mysteries. At those times I feel like an untamed, exotic animal using my bodyknowing to move sensuously through the natural world. It is then that my Inner Sex Goddess seems most alive."

I recommend reading Clarissa Pinkola Estés's superb book *Women Who Run with the Wolves* to get an even deeper feel for the wildish woman inside you, so closely akin to your Inner Sex Goddess. Both these inner archetypes—sensual, electric, and instinctual—are characterized by their strong sense of bodyknowing.

inner movies

Use the screen of your imagination to conjure up your Inner Sex Goddess. You may be surprised at who or what appears. Get comfortable. Close your eyes, breathe deeply. Relax and go inside yourself. Imagine a movie screen in your mind's eye and ask your Inner Sex Goddess to reveal herself on it. She may appear full-blown right away or slowly with a foot first and then an ankle, a leg, and so on. What does she look like? How does she dress and move? Is she a robed ancient queen or a contemporary woman in business suit over leopard-print panties? Observe her activities. Does she do different things than you do? What kind of perfume does she dab on? How does she communicate with men, verbally and nonverbally? What does she do in your workplace? at home? at school? in the neighborhood? What does she call herself—maybe she prefers Angelique to your usual Anne. Ask her how you can be more in touch with her, in a safe, elegant, and appropriate way—and how you can do this quickly and easily when need be. Request that she come to you in your dreams and teach you. Ask her to be with you when you make love with your partner and when you pleasure yourself. Thank her for revealing herself to you and give her a gift of gratitude. Let her give you a symbolic present and take careful note of what it is, for she will surely be communicating something special to you with this inner gift.

Your Inner Sex Goddess may change her appearance from day to day, too. Sometimes mine appears as a beautiful naked Greek goddess and sometimes as the Great Cosmic Yoni (in the Tantric tradition, *yoni* means "vulva"), who is the source of ecstasy, sensuality, and womanness. She has given me all sorts of symbolic presents, including a gold key (the key to any sense or experience I might want to open), a marble sculpture of a breast (representing the female qualities of nurturing and sensual beauty), and a leopard-skin G-string to remind me to be raunchy and have fun. Pat, a business executive friend of mine, says that her Inner Sex Goddess looks like Catwoman and is always admonishing her to slink around more and lick all the flavors of life. Another friend tells me that her Inner Sex Goddess looks like Marilyn Monroe, calls herself Lolita, and often shows up when she's making love to point out hidden erogenous zones on her man's body by kissing them with her red, pouty lips. My friend Georgia says that her Inner Sex Goddess is more like a colored ball of energy—sometimes pink, sometimes turquoise—that floats around Georgia's body making tingly sensations and whispering sexual secrets in her dreams.

mythological journeys

As the brilliant modern-day philosopher Joseph Campbell asserted, myths are often the key to our innermost selves, and mythological characters are the archetypes of our inner personalities. Exploring the tales of some of the mythological goddesses of sensuality can lead you to new discoveries about your own sexual persona. Of the scores of magnificent erotic deities, here are just a few to consider. Read about them, contemplate their qualities, gaze at their images, copy their poses, bring their accoutrements into your everyday life, or have inner conversations with them. Call on them just before you make love. Let them seep into your consciousness and connect you to your innermost sexual self.

Aphrodite is the Greek goddess of love, sensuality, and passionate relationships. It is she who graces your life when you fall madly in love. As the only goddess portrayed nude in Greek art, Aphrodite is proud of her beautiful nakedness and potent sexuality. In fact, in one representation of her as Aphrodite Kallipygos (Aphrodite of the Lovely Backside), she coyly draws up her robe to admire her own round fanny. The rose and lily, symbolizing the vagina, are her beloved flowers. Try draping yourself in a Grecian-style robe, even if only mentally, and lean back to gaze at your own luscious derriere. Meditate on the ripe power of this fetchingly plump piece of human art, potent enough to drive some otherwise sane men to a state of crazed desire. In emulating Aphrodite, you become a regal feminine beauty with the magical transforming power of erotic love nestled in every angle, wiggle, and curve of your body.

In the Semitic tradition, Lilith was the first woman, created at the same time as Adam. But when Adam tried to have sex with her, she grew wings and flew out of paradise to live in the desert, later becoming the bringer of agriculture and the protector of children. God then created the more compliant Eve. Let Lilith's fierce drive for sexual equality, independence, and wildness teach you about yours. Imagine yourself taking wing to escape a brand of sexuality you no longer desire and creating a powerful new one fashioned after your personal tastes and talents.

Oshun is the African Yoruba goddess of the river, sensuality, and creativity. As her waters dance sinuously through the countryside, she adorns herself with bangly stone bracelets, the beautiful clothing of the landscape, and the perfumes of the wildflowers. Also presiding over the arts, gold, and love, she provides a sensual healing balm to all who dip into her liquid body. She is completely self-contained, self-aware, and lovingly self-conscious of her natural erotic beauty as she glows in the moon's silvery romantic light. Mentally immerse yourself in her fluid sensuality and surge, ripple, and murmur like the river. Adorn yourself with flowers, flowing fabrics, and gold bracelets that jingle. Revel in your self-contained, liquid eroticism.

In the Mayan tradition, Xochiquetzal (Precious Flower) is the female deity of flowers, beauty, pleasure, and sexuality. Always joyous and free in her sensuality, she is sometimes represented as a butterfly, and her ancient worshipers often dress as hummingbirds and butterflies to dance around her rose-covered image. Merlin Stone, author of *When God Was a Woman*, says that "when a woman felt the pleasures of her body, it brought special joy to Xochiquetzal." Imagine dancing amid rose petals, hummingbird feathers, and butterfly wings as a form of ritual adoration. Worship your divine femininity by pleasuring your own fleshy rosebuds.

Shakti is a form of the Hindu Great Goddess and symbolizes the energizing life force of the universe. She is often represented as a snake, uncoiling sinuously up the human spine, awakening the life-giving, sensual energies within. Through worship of this divine goddess—which included adoring a woman's body as the goddess's human form and having sacred sex with her—male Tantric practitioners hoped to reach enlightenment. Slither like a snake and feel how this undulating movement awakens your sexual instincts. Sense the creative power of the universe uncoiling in your womb, ready to give birth to new life, new ideas, and new inner enravishments. Worship your own body as the physical manifestation of all that is divinely female—

beautiful, powerful, innately enlightened, life-nurturing, and sensual. You are the embodiment of sacred union.

I also recommend that you read Hallie Iglehart Austen's inspired and gorgeously illustrated book *The Heart of the Goddess* for poetic and practical journeys with scores of other goddesses from many cultures and time periods.

sex initiatrix

Another friend of mine likes to fantasize that she, as the officially recognized Sexiest Woman in the World, is teaching an inexperienced lover the art of pleasing a woman. Or she is a tribal sex shaman who is initiating a young boy into manhood during a sacred puberty ceremony. Or she is Sharon Stone, reducing otherwise strong men to butter simply by crossing her legs or dancing provocatively with another woman. Whether she indulges in these fantasies while standing in line at the grocery or when she is pleasuring herself or her lover, she finds it a rapid and surefire way to make her sexiest inner self come alive. And it's no wonder, for initiating virginal or emotionally unawakened men into the intoxicating mysteries of the female body is a powerful ritual we women have been performing for countless centuries. Try it and see if it doesn't awaken magic in you.

the heart of beauty

The Hawaiian shamans have a lovely way of connecting with their inner graces. They suggest finding something beautiful, like a rose or a pretty stone or a piece of yellow silk. Focus on its beauty, singling out and appreciating all the various things that make it lovely. Find the qualities it shares with you. For instance, notice the way the open petals of the rose resemble your pretty vaginal lips. Observe that the stone has many different sides, facets, and colors, like your multifaceted personality. Revel in the cool smoothness of the silk, like your satiny skin. The more you focus on the textures and senses of beauty, the more your subconscious starts to bring it into your life, the more you see it everywhere, and the more your mind and body begin to mimic these innate qualities of your Inner Sex Goddess.

the temple of erotic love

One of the most potent pathways to your inner sexual sanctum leads directly through the Jade Gate, as the Chinese call it—your vaginal opening. Though Far Eastern and Indian Tantric cultures have bestowed upon the female sexual organs poetic names like the Grotto of the White Tiger, the Honey Pot, and the Valley of Joy, modern Western culture often views them as something unclean to be hidden and ashamed of. At best, "women see their sex organs as an absence rather than a presence," laments a well-known Western gynecologist. But ancient and indigenous societies have long honored the vulva in particular as the primary source of life, pleasure, and spiritual development. Identifying it with the lotus—flower of perfection and eternity, and the great void from which all existence arises—the people of south India rubbed carved wooden yonis (vulvae) as a form of worship. Statues and paintings from South America, Africa, ninth-century Europe, and twentieth-century Australia too show goddesses displaying their sacred vulvae with authority and pride as the source of fertility, inspiration, and protection. Many of these statues appear over doorways as a reminder that the vagina is the literal gateway to life. Numerous churches and castles in the British Isles of the ninth century were thought to be sanctified by sheela-na-gigs, stone carvings of playful, smiling women with their vulvae spread wide. These peoples wisely believed, as did the tribal wizards of New Guinea, that "All magic radiates from [the vagina] as fingers do from a hand."

That kind of reverence, respect, and love for this sacred part of a woman is an essential key to releasing the Inner Sex Goddess locked inside. So, like a female Indiana

Jones on a quest for your true sexuality, you must transform what for you may be a mysterious void into a sacred temple of erotic love.

There are several ways to undertake this quest. You could make a list of all the wonderful things you can think of about your vulva—for example, as the birth canal, it's the gateway to life; men go absolutely bananas over it; it provides the highest sexual ecstasy; its many amazing talents include vast expansion, tight contraction, and copious lubrication; it is cleverly hidden; its lips are provocative protrusions or delicate wings, whatever the case may be. Make a long, sensually detailed list. Or you could practice the following meditation.

First, honor the entrance to your temple of erotic love by rubbing oils or powder on it. Place your hands over your pubic bone and vulva, feel the powerful energy that emanates from this cave of creation. As you allow the muscles in your stomach, genitals, and anus to relax, imagine that the warmth and love in your hands is being pulled into your vagina, illuminating the dark spaces and making the walls glitter with a jewellike brilliance. See this inner space being transformed into a vaulted temple, an elaborately decorated mosque, a holy shrine, a vast cathedral, or a shaman's magical cave. This is the magnificent entrance to the mysterious worlds of sexual ecstasy, sacred union, and the beginnings of life. A male friend once told me, "When you give a woman oral love, your head is cradled at the source of woman, the source of life. It's a sacred place where you can worship, and the divinity you are worshiping gives you instant feedback and the most otherworldly sensations."

Allow yourself to luxuriate in your hallowed temple of erotic love. Explore its inner recesses, discovering the sacred sensual secrets hidden there. You may want to imagine that you are one of many priestesses studying your art together or that you are performing some sexual healing for a man who has petitioned the temple goddess for rejuvenation. Learn from these activities. Ask the deity of this temple, your Inner Sex Goddess, to cleanse you of any negative feelings you may have about this sacred space and to fill it instead with reverence and love. Inquire how you may come to know her better and help her be a larger presence in your life. Just for a moment imagine that the goddess magically embodies herself in you and that you have all her knowledge, majesty, charisma, and heavenly experience. Promise her that you will always honor her temple and request that she be instantly and fully available to you whenever you merely think of this part of you. Thank her for inviting you here and gently take leave of your temple of erotic love for now. Rest in the knowledge that it and your Inner Sex Goddess are always there to nourish, support, and eroticize you.

Because I am a goddess

I will come to your

heaven, and lie on your

cloud. . . .

Let my hovel be our

heaven, let my bed be

our cloud,

On which we are united

in perfect, heavenly bliss.

—Erotic poetry of

ancient Egypt,

from <u>Sacred Sex</u>,

Robert Bates

2

creating

your

sensual

garden

the essence of being a goddess is that you transform even the most mundane events and surroundings into a celestial garden of delights by your very existence. Cultivated and in full bloom, your inner garden grows to encompass the world around you, expanding your capacity for pleasure, luring divine consorts to your domain and elevating the quality of life and lovemaking, for you and for your lover, to sublime heights. It is your Inner Sex Goddess, who, by the simple act of viewing the entire world as a sensual paradise, creates this erotic garden, first in your own life and then by divine osmosis in the lives of those around you.

Now that you recognize your inherent, natural potential as a goddess, your first divine act must be to create the sensual garden that sustains and enriches your inner life and provides a perfumed playground for all who enter it. Start by tasting the ambrosia of life, reaching out and grabbing the sensuous feeling of wind in your hair or silk on your skin, savoring the magic of a striking piece of art, reveling in the mystery of a blossoming flower, sinking into the romance of a poetic phrase or a lover's sigh. These simple yet profound acts of transformation are your natural birthright as a woman.

While men have the gift of robust action, women have

the gift of powerful perception. Sensually, men tend to focus on their genitals, whereas women are more holistic, more interested in arousing their entire bodies and their feelings. A man often wants to get right to the physical pleasure, while a woman knows how to heighten sensitivity by first creating the mood of romance. She knows that stimulating your "romance hormones" will create the context for the magic that can come from stimulating your sex hormones. In fact, many women find that if they pleasure themselves and their lovers only in a physical way, they feel bored, dishonored, and cut off from their deep feelings and true Sex Goddess nature.

At the same time, though, women intuitively understand that the physical senses are the very doorways to inner eroticism—the openings through which magic passes from the outer to the inner world and back again, the alchemical tubing that transforms sunsets, cantatas, and freshly baked bread into the hot pheromones of love. To a woman's Inner Sex Goddess, the whole world is an aphrodisiac. It's simply a matter of noticing it. And a woman becomes a Sex Goddess not by virtue of a perfect body, a bag of exotic sexual tricks, or a Valentino-like lover but by virtue of her ability to abandon herself to the electrically sensual qualities of everything around and within her and to pamper herself with them.

So if you want to make your Inner Sex Goddess a larger part of your life, use all of your senses as doorways between the exterior world and the magical interior kingdom where she dwells. See, hear, taste, smell, and feel her in every fire flame, zesty orange peel, and cat's purr. Leave room for your efficient, taking-care-of-business self, yes; she's important too. But right now, it's your sultry inner seductress that we're showering with attention. Deliberately create occasions for her to come out and play. Pamper, treat, and romance her all the time. She will turn your everyday life into a garden of sensual delights, bring your spicy inner flavors to the surface, and galvanize your man to new erotic ecstasy.

sowing the seeds of sensuality in your garden

1. Send yourself flowers. Fresh, fragrant flowers not only make you feel beautiful and adored but also provide a pretty-to-look-at and heavenly-to-smell prop for your bedroom, or for your bathroom, kitchen, or living room — wherever you decide to take your self-love tryst. Get all of your senses involved with the flowers — arrange them in a pretty vase and place them in a different spot every day; inhale their fragrance deep inside you; caress your skin with their velvety petals; garnish your food with them. Let your Inner Sex Goddess select the bouquet for its sensual appeal—two blood-red roses, one lushly fragrant gardenia, several exotic and silky tiger lilies. Get luxurious!

2. Give yourself perfume. Your favorite kind. Something that smells wickedly sexy. Spray your sheets with it. Dab it behind your ears, between your beautiful breasts, along your soft inner thighs. Smell your luscious self. One hedonistic friend of mine likes to apply a musky scent between her toes and then massage them to bring out the aroma. She says it makes her feel pampered.

3. Have plenty of romance-making candles around—tapers for elegance, votives to create a soft glow, big fat ones to help you recall phallic encounters, aromatic ones to awaken your earthy nature. Light them in the bathroom when you luxuriate in the tub. Fill your bedroom with many flames of love. Look at your gorgeous body in the mirror in shimmering candlelight. Fantasize that you're performing a magic sex ritual by candle flame and the light of the moon. Become aware of the incandescent quality of your Inner Sex Goddess. Glow.

4. Prepare a candlelight dinner for one. Set a romantic table with flowers, special dinnerware, candles, a stunning centerpiece. Indulge in aphrodisiacal appetizers such as oysters, avocados, mangoes, figs, or other juicy fruits.

Savor an entrée that you can eat with your fingers, and lick them frequently. Indulge in a sinfully rich and gooey dessert. Relish your food. Inhale its aroma. Lick it. Tear it apart with your fingers. Taste it slowly. Fruits are lovely to rub on your body and gently, slowly lick off. Don't do the dishes. Go directly to bed with yourself.

5. Treat yourself to a bottle of good wine. Red wine makes me feel much more sensuous than white or pink, but follow your own sensual urges here. A wine with a good nose will add another texture. Pour it into a delicate wineglass. Savor it. Let it slide warmly over your tongue and down your throat. Pour it on yourself and lick it off. Allow yourself to slip into the relaxed, uninhibited playground of Dionysus, the god of wine. Become his goddess consort.

6. Humanistic psychologist Abraham Maslow stated that the two most common triggers for peak experiences are music and sex. How about music and sex together? Put on some evocative music and listen to it with your whole body. My Inner Sex Goddess loves cool, sultry jazz, but other women I know prefer hot, driving salsa, romantic Mathis or Vandross, lush and elegant Ravel or Chopin, dreamy Debussy, the fireworks of Tchaikovsky, earthy blues, electric, pulsing rock, or ethereal flute music. (See the "Inner Sex Goddess Scrolls" at the back of this book for lots more specific musical suggestions.) Play whatever

turns you on at the moment. Close your eyes and slip inside the sound. Let it loosen your pelvis and shake your shoulders. Slink around in it. Sing or hum. Feel your voice vibrate your chest, throat, and face. See the colors the music creates behind your eyes. Taste its brassy, peppery, or creamy essences. Exult in the emotions it provides. Melt into the harmony of the spheres.

7. Dance. Naked. When there's no one else around to criticize your technique, your Inner Sex Goddess is free to undulate, writhe, slither, rock 'n' roll, hula, fandango, samba, or even strip to her heart's content. Close your eyes and surrender to the mood of your movement. Or dance in front of a mirror and see how sexy you look with breasts jiggling and hips swaying. Dance *with* the mirror; press up against it and feel its cool slickness against your skin. Make a hot, moist patch on it with your breath and flatten your nipple against it. Perform the dance of the seven veils with a big filmy scarf or a fringed shawl. Be provocative. Not only is this fun, loosening, limbering, and hormone-stimulating, it's also great practice for the sexy striptease you're going to do for your man someday soon.

If you feel totally uncoordinated or sexless when you dance, then try almost any other form of physical movement—yoga, aerobics, stretching to music, walking, tai chi, swimming, running. I have a shy, pixielike friend who is actually embarrassed to go to the gym because she gets overly excited by the movements of her thighs while using the StairMaster!

8. Give yourself some sexy lingerie. I love to wear lacy camisoles under my sweaters, blouses, and blazers, letting enough show so that it looks very feminine and demure but at the same time revealing and sexy as hell. My Inner Sex Goddess simply adores peekaboo lace. My friend Jennifer, on the other hand, always wears satin panties and matching plunging bras under her accounting manager pinstripe suits. She says it helps her remember she's a shameless hussy. Let your Inner Sex Goddess investigate and supplement your wardrobe. Try sleeping in a silky teddy instead of your regular oversized T-shirt. Be aware of how these textures glide and flutter over your skin. Admire yourself in a mirror often. Pose like a Victoria's Secret model. *Feel* like one. Buy and wear—if only for yourself—something that makes you look and feel like an expensive call girl. My friend Lisa, a harried mother of twin three-year-olds, says the easiest way for her to feel sexy on command is to don her see-through merry widow with lacy garters and ribbons that untie in strategic places. When she wears it with lace-top stockings and five-inch heels, she says she looks and feels deadly. Sometimes she adds her G-string silk panties. Of course, she often sports these duds for her man, but just as often she wears them only for herself.

They make her feel expensively sexy. And they become exciting props for self- or partner-lovemaking.

$9.$ Dress sensuously all the time. This does not mean you have to look overtly sexual; obviously that's not always appropriate. It means that you wear things that feel sensuous and soft; fabrics and shapes that heighten your awareness of your skin and movements. Even with your most severe business suit or your sportiest tennis togs, you can add at least one little thing, seen or unseen, that has a sensate quality to it. Silk, satin, cashmere, lace, Lycra, pearls, filmy scarves, fur, velvet, earrings that dangle against your neck, red lipstick, a push-up bra, see-through panties, a flowing skirt that billows against your bare skin, lots of bracelets, a snake armband worn on the upper arm, a wide choker, short tight skirts, silk or lace T-shirts, anything leather against your skin. Go braless. Go pantyless. Definitely go slipless, unless it's a sexy one.

It's amazing how sexy you will feel when you go without panties, particularly when you're wearing a long, flowing skirt that swishes when you walk; you're all covered up, but you feel so deliciously *exposed*. Whether your sensuous attire is demurely hidden from public view, proudly flaunted for your lover, or unabashedly admired in your own mirror, your Inner Sex Goddess will be softly vibrating and ready for further attention.

10. Soak in a hot, scented bubble bath. Spend hours at it. Read a steamy novel. Tease yourself with a soft skin brush. Bask in the glowing candlelight. Dream. Fantasize. Croon to yourself. Paint your toenails. Smooth the bubbles over your face, neck, arms, breasts, tummy, thighs, genitals. Arch your feet coquettishly and tickle your glistening toes. Massage your scalp as you wash your hair. Let the water drain while you're still in the tub. Or finish off with a cold shower. Pat yourself dry with the biggest, fluffiest towel you own. Or don't use a towel at all, and move directly into a thick terry-cloth robe. Or smooth perfumed body lotion over every inch of your skin. Float into your warm bedroom, and if there's a man in it, wake him up seductively. If not, sizzle to your own inner music.

11. Read something erotic. Curl up with a good story by Anaïs Nin and identify with the hot French coquettes she writes about. Transport yourself to another time and place where anything sexy, a little kinky, and very feminine goes. Like the women in the stories, allow yourself to be carried away by your passions until you feel that familiar warm glow begin to burn inside you. Then let your hands take it from there. There's lots of other good erotic literature out there too, something to fuel every fire, from the seductive S&M stories of A. N. Roquelaure to the taboo and poetic writing of Marco Vassi to anthologies like *Deep Down: The New Sensual Writing about Women* and *The*

Gates of Paradise. There's always Nancy Friday's *My Secret Garden* as well as many other collections of women's fantasies and even some of the letters and stories in magazines like *Playboy, Penthouse,* and *True Romance.* (See the "Inner Sex Goddess Scrolls" at the back of this book for a more complete list.) Or maybe a hot love scene from your favorite romance or trashy novel will light your inner fire. One highly organized friend of mine makes a copy of every good love scene she finds and puts it in a hot-pink file folder that she keeps locked in her nightstand drawer. Some of them are pretty dog-eared by now, but they never fail to arouse her passionate nature. Find your own favorites and keep them handy for reading to your Inner Sex Goddess or your real-life sex god.

12. Write your own erotica. Even the feel and sound of pen on paper as you write can be a sensual delight. Release your erotic feelings, hopes, and dreams onto the paper. Let your pen take flight, and follow its fanciful wanderings. Express how you felt when you last made love; recall the sensations that stirred you emotionally, sink into the feelings, and let them pour onto the paper. Invent a wildly romantic interlude in the forest, and write down exactly what you'd like to have happen. Describe a piece of music or a part of your body in sensual detail. Imagine your ideal lover and give him written instructions on how to drive you wild in bed. Tell the story of your bizarre sexual experiences on another planet. Pen an imagined page from the journal of Fanny Hill, Cleopatra, or Oshun, the river goddess. Write intensely brief poetry, cool factual journalism, or hot turgid prose. Create a passionate romance novel or a porn comic book. Try on different writing styles to suit your mood or to create a new one. Since no one will be grading this paper, really let yourself go. Don't be afraid to dig down deep inside you and reveal your heart's secret erotic desires.

A single real estate broker I know told me she once spent a lone day at the beach feeling the blazing sun on her skin and fantasizing about a hot lover who would sneak up and inflame her body even further with steamy kisses. Later, feeling compelled to pour her sensual feelings onto paper, she wrote a rhymeless poem describing her fantasy love fest. She said that concentrating on finding the right words helped her relive and enhance the experience, and rereading it now and then recaptures all those sizzling skin sensations and simmering passions. Her poem turned out to be one of her most treasured personal turn-ons.

13. Ogle sexy pictures. Your Inner Sex Goddess is much more visually erotic than you might imagine, so give yourself permission to open the optic channels to your libido. She loves those bare-chested men in Calvin Klein ads, lovers in the ecstatic embraces and wild positions depicted so beautifully in Oriental woodcuts and Indian miniatures,

pictures of luscious babes who look rather like you in men's magazines, beefcake postcards (one woman I know collects a few eye-poppers in every town she visits), hunky-man calendars (my calendar for this year happens to be "The Men of Hawaii," and are they hot!), nude photos you've taken of your lover, the sexually explicit drawings found in *The Joy of Sex* and other sex instruction books, museum postcard reproductions of beautifully sculpted nude Greek statues, the cover of a steamy novel, magazine photos of movie stars in action. Actually, some of the most erotic images I've ever seen are photographs or paintings of nature — Georgia O'Keeffe's paintings of flowers that look like women's vulvae; beautifully rendered still lifes where the soft fruit or flowers resemble swollen lips, rounded breasts, or plump behinds; photos of dense redwood forests exuding damp earthiness and phallic sensuality; drawings of curvy, openly inviting shells glistening with moisture.

Collect your personal preferences and keep them at the ready in your erotic file folder. Drool and fantasize to your libido's content. Imagine you are *in* the picture, and follow your bliss.

14. Watch X-rated videos. Yes, real women watch porn flicks. In fact, your Inner Sex Goddess can literally be transfigured by visual eroticism. One of the best descriptions I've ever heard of this phenomenon was reported by Sallie Tisdale in her fabulous book *Talk Dirty to*

Me: "Watching my first adult movie, watching for the first time a man penetrate another woman, was like leaving my body all at once. I was outside my body, watching, because she on the screen above me *was* me; and then I was back in my body very much indeed. My lust was aroused as surely and uncontrollably by the sight of sex as hunger can be roused by the smell of food."

Adult videos are much improved these days, and often you don't even have to fast-forward to get past all the boring or stupid stuff. For sleek erotic atmosphere with gorgeous men and women, try Andrew Blake's films. Candida Royale and her Femme Productions put out many sexy films that are more romantic and woman-centered. These and many other modern hard-, soft-, and medium-core porn videos (see "The Inner Sex Goddess Scrolls" for a more complete list) provide a great tool for expanding your sexual horizons and acting out vicariously what you might never do in real life. Whether you're into fantasizing about vampires, whips, bisexuality, group scenes, or just plain sizzling sex and plenty of it, there's a film made just for you. Your Inner Sex Goddess can also learn some interesting new tricks to try by yourself or with a partner. As my fiftyish friend Judy said when she loaned me one of her favorites, "I thought the film was trash, but it made me laugh, think, and swoon all at the same time. I couldn't wait to plug in my vibrator." I recommend that you (1) read the package carefully to get a feel for how kinky, outlandish, or romantic the film is; (2) trade videos and personal reviews of them with friends; (3) watch alone at first; and (4) watch with a vibrator in your lap.

 15. Collect, admire, and play with erotic objects. Joanna, my plain but profoundly charismatic soul sister, likes to collect phallic objects, for instance. Her favorite is a two-inch-long crystal penis, every detail true to life. Obviously too small to do anything with, this toy is just for her Inner Sex Goddess to fantasize over. I have a stunning satinwood statue of a man arching over a woman's shoulder to kiss her breast; I love to gaze at it and stroke it. My pleasingly plump friend Marsha collects beautifully tasteful representations of women's pelvises and derrieres; they make her feel good about her own. Another friend likes lots of velvet pillows for looking, touching, and rubbing against sensitive body parts. Some women find that certain wild animals and the coiled power they represent arouse sexual thoughts—panthers, snakes, and stallions, for instance—and they enjoy having pictures, statuettes, or stuffed toys of these creatures around to inspire, admire, and pet. Pretty feathers, and even feathery plants, can be a sensual delight for the eyes and skin. Having a fetish for erotic collectibles not only results in some fabulous toys for your lovemaking lair but also keeps your sensual self alive and tantalized all the time, always on the lookout for a new addition to your secret sensitizing collection.

16. Aroma is another powerful stimulus for your Inner Sex Goddess. In fact, the ancient Egyptians, believing that fragrant oils were created by the gods, used scents to evoke in themselves the joyous sensuality of Hathor or the powerful regenerative qualities of Isis, for instance. Unleash your inner goddesses by inhaling deeply of *all* the "essential oils" of life—ocean air, baking bread, freshly washed hair, damp earth, baby skin, lemon peel, the musky aroma of sex, and especially flowers and their liquid essences. The lush smell of white ginger instantly unlocks all my voluptuous instincts, so I always return from Hawaii with ginger sachets to tuck in my drawers and pillows. Try placing a drop of your favorite essential oil on a bedside lightbulb or on melting wax as it drips down the side of a candle. Spray gardenia perfume in your linen closet and later unfold the fragrance onto your bed. Dip a cotton ball in jasmine oil and nestle it between the mounds of your breasts. Bathe in lavender-scented water. Saturate a lacy white handkerchief with ylang-ylang oil, wear it next to your skin for a while, and then carelessly leave it lying around in one of your man's favorite haunts.

17. Burn incense. A room filled with the heady aroma of musk, rose, jasmine, ylang-ylang, or amber, one of my favorites, somehow oozes sensuality. Like the ancient Tantricas, use the pungent smoke of your favorite incense to activate and eroticize your chakras (energy centers). Hold a stick of burning incense near your pubic bone and then move it slowly up the front of your body all the way to the top of your head, pausing for a few moments at your genitals, diaphragm, heart, and throat. Keep the incense about two inches away from your skin. Somehow this raises your sexual temperature and infuses your body and mind with heat, preparing you for an unusually sensual experience.

18. Develop an eye for the erotic qualities of nature. Women are especially talented at seeing and feeling the sensuous beauty in a vivid sunset, a purple craggy mountain at dawn, frothy ocean waves, emerald green rolling hills, tall grasses rippling in the wind, a certain iridescence of light and shade in the forest. Feel the thickness or sweetness of the air at the beach, in the mountains, in a forest glade, in the steamy jungle. Smell and taste it. Gardeners know that massaging wet dirt can be a sensuous experience. Caress the tender petals of a flower. Eat a blade of grass. Close your eyes and let the sound of crashing ocean waves wash over your body. Trickle hot sand over your feet and legs. Press your body against the rough bark of a tree. Walk barefoot in the grass. Feel with your eyes as you watch a horse run, a cat stretch, a bird soar, a snake slither, a butterfly float, a tiger spring, or a dragonfly mate.

If you live in the city and can't get away, take your Inner Sex Goddess to a museum or art gallery and let her drink in the sensual images of nature depicted in fine works of art. Luxuriate in Monet's sumptuous gardens or John Constable's overpowering, detailed landscapes. Absorb the subtleties of light or merge with the stillness in a photograph. Become intimate with Ansel Adams and his stunning black-and-white adorations of canyons and deserts. Imagine yourself into the setting of a van Gogh and let your animal senses run wild.

19. Mine your past for experiences and sensations that touch off interior sparks. Old love letters, postcards, snapshots, prom mementos, valentines, love songs, discarded clothing of his and yours, and even photos of a magnificent beach you went to by yourself are a living treasure chest of evocative sense triggers. Close your eyes and submerge yourself completely in the sights, sounds, and smells associated with that memory. Feel his arms around your waist as you danced to that old song; taste the souvlaki and baklava from that romantic trip to the Greek islands; drink in the smell of his skin when he wore that old flannel shirt. Vividly recall the rapid beating of your heart and the warm tingle under your skin that burned these moments into the very fibers of your body. Your Inner Sex Goddess lives in those vibrant sense memories.

20. As a little girl, you knew the power of your mother's lipstick and high heels to transform you into a sexy, grown-up chick; or a clown's hat to bring out your

silly oaf side; or a bandanna and a stick for a horse to turn you into a Wild West cowgirl. This stuff still works, even on your fuddy-duddy adult self, because Your Inner Sex Goddess adores the game of dress-up. Try on any persona that excites your erotic imagination and act the role to the hilt in front of your private mirror. Adorn yourself like a tart: net stockings, garter belt showing beneath short tight skirt, five-inch heels, brightly rouged cheeks, and teased hair. Wriggle your behind, whip your handbag around, expose your push-up bra and crotchless panties, and stand disdainfully arched against the doorway to attract imaginary customers. Dress up like a harem girl, with floating sheer scarves, beaded vest, lots of jangling jewelry, ankle bracelets, heavy Cleopatra eyeliner, and face veil. Pull the scarves provocatively across your breasts and through your legs; with head down, peek out from behind your veil with inviting eyes; let your scarves and ropes of jewelry fly out from your body as you twirl, dance, and undulate. Or be a demure geisha and don a kimono, wide silk sash, chopsticks in your piled-up hair, and the whitest makeup you can find. Geishas consider the nape of the neck very erotic, and they extend their white makeup around to the back of the neck, making a long, pointed pattern with it in the space where their kimono collar falls away. Step mincingly about the room, flutter your fan in strategic places, purse your lips, and enticingly caress your brazenly exposed neck and ankles. Or transform yourself into a hula dancer by baring your breasts, tying a sarong or big scarf low around your hips, and arranging flowers and leaves in your hair. Sway your hips, raise your arms gracefully to one side, and perform the sensuous *ami* movement by rotating your hips around in one big continuous circle. Slip into the memory of how you looked and felt, or take your harem scarf or your net stockings to bed with you, the next time you want to entice your Inner Sex Goddess or your consort lover.

21. Try the practice of vivification. The Native Americans believed that everything—rocks, trees, streams, animals, clouds—had a living spirit, and they addressed each one with the same respect, awe, and love they would give to any divine being. When you become conscious of every flower, shell, fig, painting, or piece of music as a living essence of sensuality, its vital spark will come alive for you, revealing all its rich colors, secret smells, and soul-tingling textures. And in getting to know this voluptuous being, you will be transformed. As Joseph Campbell said, "The [self] that sees a 'thou' is not the same [self] that sees an 'it.'"

your body: the temple within the garden

We don't need to attend a sex seminar, travel to an exotic locale, or search out the perfect lover to open wide the doors of our true sensuality. All we have to do is be fully present right here in the sacred temple of our own bodies. As the Boston Women's Health Collective has so brilliantly put it, "Our Bodies *Are* Ourselves" (emphasis mine). Through the senses of our bodies we know the world and ourselves. Through our bodies we *know*. We know what we want and need. We know what we feel. We know what to do. We know who we are. We know ourselves as women. In fact, the poet Adrienne Rich has written that women "think through the body."

By becoming more aware of our bodies, bringing our attention to each part as we observe or touch it, we tap into the deep wisdom contained in these our miraculous sensate morsels of flesh. We begin to learn the language of our instincts, which direct and guide us when we make love. All too often, though, we let our heads take the lead in bed and leave our wise bodily instincts behind. This separates us from our full sensuality and leaves us feeling unfulfilled, as though something were still lacking. It is! What's missing is the full experience of the senses we are trying so hard to stimulate, and the powerful sensate wisdom of our bodies. So often we criticize, ignore, or try to change our bodies. But without them, how could we have the wonder that is sex and sensuality?

Your Inner Sex Goddess knows that in order to be a great lover, with your man or with yourself, to enjoy lovemaking and discover new sexual delights every day, you have to be fully present in your body. You have to revere it as the sacred temple of your sensuality and consciously inhabit all of its rooms, hallways, and turrets. So when you want to tempt the voluptuousness out of your bones or turn your lover into hot mush, start by taking the time to consciously inhabit the temple of your body. Turn your mental switch from outer visual mode to inner sensate mode. Really *feel* the sensations of your skin. John Gray, author of *Men Are from Mars, Women Are from Venus,* says that women have more "cuddling hormones" than men and that the skin all over their bodies is ten times more sensitive than men's, as sensitive as the skin on a man's penis. So take advantage of those extra pleasure sensors. Concentrate on the tingles, the tickles, the heat rising and falling, the waves of pleasure. Luxuriate in your body. Here are some things you can do to increase your awareness and turn on your body senses.

22. Rub your hands together rapidly for about ten seconds before you touch your body. This (1) brings your awareness to your hands and the physicalness of your body, (2) sensitizes your hands, (3) makes them nice and warm, (4) creates energy that you will definitely feel when you touch your hands to your body. Watch out for tingles!

23. Close your eyes and take several slow, deep breaths. Feel the breath traveling to every corner of your body. Let it tingle. Imagine that you are breathing in through your breasts and nipples. Let them become filled with heat and energy. Focus intently on the subtle sensations and a new sense of presence in your breasts. Then imagine breathing in through your vagina. Again, really concentrate your attention there. Feel its fullness, warmth, and energy.

24. Another sensitizing breath technique that comes from the Tantric tradition is called the Breath of Fire. Sit up straight and pant very fast and very hard. Make a hissing sound as you inhale and exhale. Continue this for about fifteen seconds (you can work up to two minutes, but take it slowly at first). Then inhale very deeply, hold your breath for a count of five, and exhale fully and slowly. As its name suggests, this technique will ignite your sexual fires; and if you want to direct them to a specific place in your body, you can do so simply by focusing your attention there as you perform your final slow exhalation. Feel the hot inner breath actually traveling to your favorite erotic hot spot.

25. During rhythmic activities like running, rowing, singing, and making love, people's breathing will often synchronize. If you consciously model your breathing pattern after the excited panting or deep moaning rhythms of peak sex, you will find your body and mind responding with the physical sensations of arousal, even releasing titillating pheromones.

26. Contract every muscle in your body as tightly as you can for five seconds. All at the same time, clench your fists, hunch your shoulders, curl your toes, pull in your stomach, tighten your leg and arm muscles, scrunch your eyelids shut. Contract everything. Then release your tension completely for five seconds. Do this five times. Finally, relax, relax, relax. Let go. See what happens.

27. Lick yourself all over. Start by sliding your tongue across the tips of your fingers. Then travel down to lap your palm, encircle your wrist with a wet tongue, lick the back of your hand and your knuckles, trace a tongue line down your forearm with occasional nibbles along the way, and flick your tongue in the hollow of your elbow. Continue languorously over the rest of your body. When you are with your lover, ask him to join you by licking and biting your other arm.

28. Sensitize your head by massaging your scalp or by shampooing your hair while imagining that a lover is doing it, brushing your hair for a long time, pulling slowly on your earlobes, tracing circles on your scalp with your fingernails, pressing the hollows beside your eyes and behind your ears, tapping your head all over with your fingertips, rubbing your scalp with a rough towel. Close your eyes and let these physical tingles awaken the sensual you.

29. Bathe in the hot sun—nude, if possible. Sunlight actually increases the level of the hormone androgen, the female counterpart of testosterone, filling your body with delicious liquid desire and bringing your Inner Sex Goddess to life.

30. My friend Gloria has developed a simple but elegant way to be deeply in touch with the sensations of her body. She says that when her erotic feelings first start to blossom, the bottoms of her feet start to tingle. She then focuses on moving that tingle up to her vagina, or wherever she wants it, and she moves and breathes in ways that keep that prickle of excitement growing, no matter what else may follow. Whatever your body's calling cards of arousal are—tingling feet, melting chest muscles, burning palms,

soft tongue—focus on those sensations and visualize them expanding into your fingers, breasts, pelvis, toes, head, wherever. Feel them actually traveling along your nerve pathways, glowing, heating, and thrilling your entire body.

31. Rub your skin with fur, velvet, chamois, felt, honey, olive oil, cold cream, rough facial cleansing cream, suede, cold cans of soda, fresh porcini (wild mushrooms whose firm silkiness feels like the skin on the tip of your man's penis). Stand in the rain, run through the wind, dip your hands in snow, submerge yourself in a cool, bubbling brook. Lie naked on a rug, a wooden floor, the sand, a bed of leaves. Ask your Inner Sex Goddess what her favorite skin treat is and indulge yourself with it.

32. Sensuously apply perfumed lotion to your entire body. Don't forget the backs of your knees, your underarms, the nape of your neck. Really focus on the physical sensations as you do this—the place where you are rubbing, your hands as they caress your skin, the heady aroma. Be aware of every one of the millions of nerve endings all over your skin.

33. Give yourself a massage. It's a good idea to trim your nails first so you can use your fingertips without getting stabbed. Take your time and be very sensuous about it. Slather yourself with oil, scented or unscented. As you move your hands over your body, focus your attention on the delicious sensations that are exchanged between fingers and skin, each experiencing its own distinct pleasures. Start at your feet and slowly work your way up your legs and torso, leaving your genitals for last. Or begin with your face and scalp and work your way down. Spend lots of time on your fingers and hands because they are extremely sensitive to touch and because they take quite a beating during your busy day. Use long, sensuous strokes that go deep into the skin, or work in soothing circular motions. Large, two-handed circles over the tummy are especially nice. Let your hands discover all those little knots of tension, and knead them out. Cup your hands over your eyes, breasts, and pubic bone. Caress, hold, and cradle your body the way a lover would.

34. As you are performing number 32 or 33, do the following body awareness exercise. If you have started with your foot, for instance, close your eyes and "listen" to the sensate messages your foot is sending you. How does it feel? Does it want stronger or gentler pressure? Lift your hands for a moment and be aware that the foot you have stroked probably feels lighter and more vibrant than your other foot. As you massage your foot, tell it how beautiful and strong it is, and thank it for supporting you so well. Let your foot drink in all this pleasure. Continue in the same manner with every part of your body.

We human beings are able to make love more frequently and sensuously than perhaps any other animal. Yet we are often disappointed after lovemaking. Why? Because most of us are like owners of a precious Stradivarius violin that we have never learned to play.

—Jolan Chang, *The Tao of the Loving Couple*

3

self-pleasuring— the key to the kingdom

As a sacred temple, your body is the divine instrument of pleasures fit for the gods. And before you can use it to make beautiful music with your partner, you have to become a virtuoso on your own Stradivarius. In order to seduce others with your heavenly melodies, you must first seduce yourself by drawing out your deep, wild sexuality, turning on the magnetic firelight of your body, and inflaming your own delicious passion. Even the gods and goddesses of ancient Egypt obeyed this basic rule, for among them it is said that the sun brought the world into existence by first pleasuring itself. After that, it was the female sky who, by lowering her beautiful potent body over the male earth, created the union that produced life.

Autoeroticism has long been practiced as a natural and elegant way of honoring the glorious gift of a body and communing with one's inner divinity—from primitive cave drawings of masturbation to the erotic dildos found in ancient Egyptian tombs, to a Buddhist temple in Orissa that boasts beautiful bas-reliefs of men and women stroking themselves. Even today's sex therapists extol the benefits of autoeroticism as a vital tool for self-knowledge and relationship-enhancement, professing that sexual virtuosity with a lover is attained by first becoming a sexual virtuoso with yourself. Many ordinary women bear this out; they have told me that, despite the fact that their first experience with lovemaking was merely okay or even disappointing, they later learned to reach sexual heights and become extraordinary lovers by focusing on sensualizing their own bodies. Such was the case with me.

my story

I had a very strict and sheltered upbringing that did not include getting information about sex, although I always suspected that something mysterious, powerful, and potentially dangerous or enjoyable (both equally discouraged) lurked beneath the currents of everyday life. During high school I necked and petted with my boyfriends, but genital contact was so out of the question that I didn't even think about it. Then, finally, at age nineteen, I had intercourse for the first time—a somewhat boring encounter with a steady boyfriend that produced the required bloody sheet, but not much in the way of passion, excitement, or romance. Subsequent boyfriends helped me see that sex could be sexier than had been apparent in the first encounter, but my eyes weren't truly opened to the sensuality and power I owned for myself (and with which I could light all sorts of flashing sparks in men) until several years later when I bought a vibrator.

A trusted friend had raved about the fun she was having with her mechanical instrument of pleasure, and I wanted to explore too. Suddenly I could concentrate fully on my own body and the delicious inner and outer feelings I was having without having a man's wants and needs to worry about. And because the vibrator was so intense and indefatigable, and because it would stay exactly where I wanted it to, I found myself making a discovery: "Oh, *that's* what an orgasm is!" Over the next several months I explored every inch of my body and learned to love my hips, little toes, breasts, inner elbows, genitals, and earlobes for the voluptuous and powerful way they could make me feel. I gave up feeling embarrassed or ashamed about any of my body's shortcomings, and even about the fact that it could give me such pleasure. In fact, learning about my own personal poetry gave me greater self-esteem, zest, and natural charm. And the more I enjoyed my own body, the hotter and sexier I felt, the better lover I became, and the more men seemed to be attracted to me. That's why, when women say to me,

"I have a really great lover. Why would I want to play with myself?"

"If I masturbate, it means I can't get a lover and have to settle for second best."

"I already know how to massage my hot button. Who needs anything else?"

"My man feels too threatened by my vibrator."

"I masturbate every once in a while, but it's kinda boring."

"I'm afraid I'll get so aroused by women's bodies I'll become a lesbian."

"Isn't that really more for men?"

"I could never do *that!*"

"I don't really know how."

"I'm not oversexed!" . . .

I say that you can settle for good sex or even pretty great sex if you want to, but I believe that self-loving is one of the most vital keys to your inner kingdom of abandoned, expert, and rapturous sexuality. It's certainly one of the easiest, fastest, and most reliable ways to unleash your Inner Sex Goddess. And if you want some sensible, virtuous reasons to spend precious time and energy on what may seem like frivolous, threatening, or wickedly self-indulgent pleasures, here they are.

Reason # 1

Self-Pleasuring Is the Single Most Important Thing You Can Do to Become a Truly Great Lover.

By focusing on your own total fulfillment, you gain access to the complete you—the savage you, the loving you, the lusty trampy you, the giving you, the unbridled you, the inventive and adventurous you, the magnetic you, the Aphrodite you, the instinctive wild you, the Sex Goddess you. You discover a whole new way of being a woman.

You have the keys to your body, your physical and emotional sensations, and your most lascivious libido. Self-pleasuring allows you to find out firsthand:

- What most turns you on — or off
- What makes you feel less inhibited
- What feels good real slow and gentle or very hard and fast
- How long you like to be stimulated
- How sensitive your nipples and clitoris are
- Where your G-spot is and how it likes to be rubbed
- The best way for you to reach orgasm
- How to extend your sexual capacity into multiple orgasmic bliss

By becoming familiar with your sexual organs and the pleasure they can provide, you discover just how beautiful and powerful they really are; your genitals may even become your favorite feature. I know a woman who feels that her pink flowerlike inner vaginal lips are one of her strongest assets. She says men are fascinated with her large fleshy petals and want to stroke and kiss them end-lessly!

When you discover and awaken all of your personal hot spots and habits, when you find out for yourself what the tight contractions of your vagina feel like to a man, when you see how sexy you look with hips undulating, nipples erect, and in the full throes of orgasm, you have a visceral experience of the high-wattage sexual power that is yours to command, enjoy, and give. You *know* you are a deliciously dangerous weapon of love.

And when you're in firm control of all your rich sexual assets and weapons, needing nothing outside yourself, yet wanting and commanding the whole world of sensuality, you are prepared to fully inflame your man's body, his mind, and that most powerful erogenous zone of all—his imagination.

Reason #2

Self-Pleasuring Makes You *Feel* Sexy.

In *203 Ways to Drive a Man Wild in Bed,* I explained that the first secret of great sex is *"Feel* sexy, and you will *be* sexy." One of the fastest, surest, and most enjoyable ways to summon up that sense of power and sensuality is to titillate your body and mind with some self-loving.

That's because thinking about sex makes you feel sexy; preparing to have sex makes you feel sexy; knowing and appreciating your body makes you feel sexy; loving your genitals makes you feel sexy; seeing how beautiful you look when you are flushed with excitement makes you feel sexy; orgasm makes you feel sexy. And stimulating your sex hormones makes you feel sexy; that is, after all, their physiological function—to engorge your womb with blood, to start your vaginal juices flowing, to activate the sensation-rich nerve endings in your genitals and breasts, to stiffen your nipples, to flush your skin with extra blood and energy. In fact, the electromagnetic energy field surrounding your body begins to overflow with sexual energy and potency.

In fact, self-pleasuring actually expands your capacity for pleasure. The more pleasure you get, the more you want. The more you learn to enjoy, the more you can handle. It's like when you finally try the Flying Teacup ride at the carnival: you get off feeling giddy and exhilarated. *Now* you are ready to take on the Giant Killer Roller Coaster! Building the pleasure of sex and sensuality is similar. All of your senses come alive, expand, and reach enthusiastically for more.

And most important, being in touch with your Inner Sex Goddess makes you feel sexy. She is the repository of all your sensual drives, feelings, and knowledge. When you respect and love her and give her free rein to express herself, she will reward you with the riches of your own natural sexual power and artistry. Your Inner Sex Goddess *knows* how to feel and be sexy. She *is* sex.

Reason #3

Self-Pleasuring Puts You in Touch with Your Body.

We ignore our bodies most of the time. We're too busy organizing complex work and social schedules, we're devising five-year plans and household budgets, we're weighing the pros and cons of buying a new refrigerator or a new dress, we're making decisions and formulating opinions, we're determining if a new man is safe, mature, and stable enough to go to bed with. We even make physical exercise a rigorous mental obsession, calculating our heart rates and personal best scores. We tend to view the input and sensations of our bodies as less important, less reliable, and less real than those of our minds. But this separation of mind and body can be terribly self-destructive.

I find that when I neglect the pleasures of self-loving I become more critical of my body. I see it as a separate entity with cottage cheese thighs and wrinkles around the eyes. I lose a nurturing awareness of the rhythms and cycles of my body and of nature. I don't know and love myself as well. I start feeling powerless and depressed.

But a luxurious session of self-play can quickly restore my feelings of oneness with body and soul. It can do the same for you. By focusing your attention on the sensations of your skin, muscles, and seemingly countless erogenous zones and by feeling your womanness intensely, you come to know your body again and love all of its pleasures. You may find you actually like your fleshy thighs and crinkly eyes; they too are full of sweet sensations. Your body, mind, and soul begin resonating together once again. You feel healthier, earthier, more in tune with yourself, more human. Your body lets you in on its inherent playfulness and love of dancing, exercising, and making love. You reclaim the joy of being alive, and you feel glad to have your sensuous female body, which was made for pleasure.

Reason #4

Self-Pleasuring Strengthens and Increases the Flexibility of Your Love Muscle.

In case you don't already know it, the pubococcygeus (PC) is your primary love muscle. It's the one you use to stop the flow of urine, and if it's well trained, you can use it to massage a man's penis to ecstasy. It is also the muscle in which you experience most of the contractions of orgasm, and if you keep it well toned, it helps you have bigger, better, and more frequent orgasms. Just flexing it can make you feel sexy and hot. That's why having a strong and flexible PC muscle is crucial to great sex, whether you're flying in tandem or solo.

The increased blood supply and toning contractions of orgasm vitalize your PC muscle. It feels good if it's exercised and strengthened, and then it pays you back by giving you better climaxes and more control of your partner's pleasure too. And of course the easiest way to give yourself plenty of lovely toning orgasms—unless your man is available for hot sex twenty-four hours a day—is by self-pleasuring.

Reason #5

Self-Pleasuring Teaches You How to Have Orgasms—Lots of Them—Easily and Quickly.

Many women have never had an orgasm with or without a partner. Many are not sure if they have or not. Many women fake it just to keep the peace or to avoid hurting his feelings. According to recent surveys, only about 30 percent of women have orgasms through intercourse alone, but 80 to 99 percent achieve climax with masturbation. This is astonishing. It's completely normal and very common *not* to have an orgasm through intercourse all by itself. Most women need additional stimulation to experience their full sexual potential and enjoyment, but all the while they think they're supposed to be climaxing all over the place just from their lover's penis. While some women do, most do not. The truth is that once you learn how and where your body needs to be stimulated in order to have an orgasm, you can start having them any time you want to, easily and quickly—during intercourse, while masturbating with your partner, and through self-pleasuring on your own.

A woman's body is an amazing pleasure machine, capable of trillions of orgasms, big ones and small ones. In fact, according to Dr. Andrew Stanway in *The Art of Sensual Loving*, "any one woman's total sexual output through her life (intercourse plus self-produced orgasms) is probably more than a man's." It seems that a woman's capacity for sexual gratification is nearly limitless. And the more orgasms you have, the more your body learns to respond to all types of stimulation so that it is easier to have more and more wonderful climaxes.

The best way to teach your body to have easy orgasms is through self-pleasuring. You can try out all kinds of fun things in complete privacy, without having to worry if you're taking too much time, looking silly, or doing something incredibly weird. If you find it takes twenty minutes of constant clitoral massage to make you come, then you've discovered a great secret. If you learn that pulling on your nipples or massaging your anus while you thrust your finger in and out of your love tunnel throws you over the edge, then you've found the key to unlocking your orgasmic bliss. Chances are, you are not going to discover these things while having sex with your man. You'll be too embarrassed to explore yourself or too busy worrying about his pleasure, or you won't have enough time because he's already had his orgasm and gone to sleep. Stop denying yourself! Use your hands to teach your body how to have its ultimate pleasure.

Reason #6

Self-Pleasuring Puts You in Control of Your Own Pleasure.

When you know your body and its sexual responses really well, *you* can control whether, when, and how to have your orgasm. You know just what it takes to create warm liquid feelings throughout your entire body and to bring on those delicious orgasmic contractions. Then you can guide your man to help you have *multiple* orgasms, if that's your desire. The point is that you know exactly what you want and need, and you know precisely how to achieve it. You are your own mistress.

And then there are times when you don't have a man in your life. Fortunately that doesn't mean you have to give up being your Sex Goddess self, because while you are self-pleasuring you can fantasize the most outrageous encounters, imagining every single touch, kiss, and stroke being done exactly the way you want it, for as long as you want it, as tenderly or roughly as you want it, by whomever you desire. Your imaginary sex partner anticipates your every sexual wish and never tires of titillating you all the way to the outside edge of your pleasure envelope. I've had several lovely liaisons with a fantasy Mel Gibson, for instance, where he licked me all over for three hours, massaged and kissed my breasts just the way I like it for about an hour and a half, and then made hard and fast love to me for forty-five minutes without stopping till we both collapsed in luscious exhaustion.

And even when you do have a man in your life, he will sometimes be away, ill, or just not into it. Again, your own loving hands are always there to do your bidding. Sometimes your man may be just plain tired out from having given you ten star-burst orgasms in a row, but you want eleven that night. On those occasions you always have the ability to continue riding the waves on your own. In other words, you are not at the mercy of a partner's sexual whims, skill, or presence to enjoy your own ecstasies.

Reason #7

Self-Pleasuring Leads to Self-Confidence in All Areas of Life.

When you know how to turn yourself on and realize that you can do so anytime without depending on anyone else, you will gain a tremendous sense of self-control and self-confidence. You feel surer of yourself, more deserving, and more powerful.

This exhilarating sense of potency naturally spreads to other areas of your life. Learning to take responsibility for your own sensual enjoyment gives you the confidence to take the same initiative elsewhere. The aliveness and power you feel as a self-created Sex Goddess help you know that you are a fascinating and limitlessly capable creature, regardless of the role you are playing at the moment. My banker friend Charlotte says, "Now that I'm in touch with my full range of feelings and experiences, I am more complete, more integrated. I know the amazing things I'm capable of in all areas of my life. And I like myself for it."

According to research cited by Lonnie Barbach in *For Yourself*, "consistently orgasmic women tend to describe themselves as contented, good-natured, insightful, self-confident, independent, realistic, strong, capable, and understanding while non-orgasmic women tend to describe themselves as bitter, despondent, dissatisfied, distrustful, fussy, immature, inhibited, prejudiced, and sulky." Gee, I'd rather be around a frequently orgasmic woman. Wouldn't you? And so would your husband or lover, your children, your co-workers, and your friends. You become an asset to the rest of the world when you are happy, strong, and fulfilled. And you know it.

Reason #8

Self-Pleasuring Is the Key to Overcoming Sexual Guilt and Self-Repression.

The more time you spend getting to know your body—feeling comfortable with it and all the wonderful things it can do for you and seeing how beautiful it is at rest and during all stages of excitement—the more you come to understand that sexual pleasure is a natural and especially wonderful benefit of living in a body. Our bodies love to be stroked and caressed; they thrive on it. In fact, if deprived of physical affection they can become ill.

Finding out that self-pleasuring is a natural and beautiful function, something that makes you feel great about yourself and more loving to those around you, frees you from all that guilt you may have been carrying around. It breaks down the walls of inhibition and helps you let go of the fears and musty old taboos that have been keeping you from fully enjoying your natural Sex Goddesshood. And once you do release whatever sexual guilt is lurking in all those dark inner corners, you will be able to express your sexuality and your true self more freely—*with* your lucky lover. You can start enjoying sex more and regretting it less.

Reason #9

Self-Pleasuring Promotes Health, Well-Being, and Energy.

Your sex muscles are not isolated. To paraphrase an old song, "The sex bone's connected to the thigh bone; the thigh bone's connected to the back bone," and so forth. Healthy, well-toned pelvic and vaginal muscles lead to healthy, well-toned stomach muscles, leg muscles, and on and on. To say nothing of the increased flow of blood and energy that permeates your entire body when you indulge in a vigorous self-pleasuring workout. Exercise makes for healthy, happy muscles. It also boosts your energy production and releases endorphins that create a sense of well-being. In fact, according to Dr. Deepak Chopra, a chemical called Interleukin-2 floods the body during any positive exhilarating activity—and I think most of us will agree that sizzling self-play qualifies as such an activity. Interleukin-2 is a powerful anticancer neuropeptide, the body's chemical equivalent to a feeling of joy. So for a quick mental and physical pick-me-up that will also build long-term health—some women say it even makes them feel younger—indulge in your favorite form of self-play.

Reason #10

Self-Pleasuring Reduces Stress and Tension.

The intense muscular and emotional release of self-induced orgasm provides quite a tonic for anxiety, tense muscles, job stress, traffic jam tension, or the frustration of a bad hair day. Stress and tension restrict the flow of blood and energy through your body and cause blocks to creativity, good health, and joyful living. Like a good massage, self-pleasuring can soothe and release these tensions with the simple touch of a finger. My friend Diane, who has a very stressful job, says, "I sometimes masturbate every day if it's a tough work week. I don't know how I'd manage the stress caused by intense days filled with frantic meetings and impossible deadlines without it!"

Reason #11

Self-Pleasuring Helps You Sleep.

On those nights when your mind is racing, or you're all keyed up from some intense conversation or event, or worry is keeping your eyes glued to the ceiling, you can invite the Sandman into your bed by indulging in some stress-releasing self-massage. It has been scientifically proven that giving yourself a lovely orgasm relaxes your muscles and tunes your brain waves to alpha (the brain waves of dreaming sleep and creativity) or even theta (deep sleep). And it's a "sleeping pill" that has no side effects and will leave you energized, not stupefied, in the morning.

Reason #12

You Don't Have to Stop Feeling Good When You or Your Sex Organs Are in a Delicate Condition.

Suppose that you have an infection, you've recently had non-womb-related surgery, you are in the last stages of pregnancy, you just gave birth, or you are having your period. These are times when it might not be comfortable, desirable, or safe to indulge in love play with a partner. But during such times, you usually need *more* loving, not less. During those times, you could really use the recuperative magic of sensual bliss. Fortunately, you can always give yourself just the right gentle caresses and love strokes to soothe your soul and keep you in life-affirming touch with your Inner Sex Goddess.

Reason #13

For Older Women, Self-Pleasuring Increases Vaginal Lubrication and Lessens the Discomfort of Dryness.

This is true not just when you are pleasuring yourself, but all the time. By keeping your vaginal glands active, before, during, and after the menopausal years, you are encouraging them to produce more lubrication regularly. So you'll be juicier for your man too. When you keep your vaginal muscles contracting and those hormones secreting, you'll stay sexually active and in touch with your Inner Sex Goddess.

Reason # 14

Self-Pleasuring Provides Relief from Menstrual Cramps.

One of the benefits of having nicely toned and frequently orgasmic vaginal muscles is that they are stronger, more elastic, and much better able to handle the inner movements associated with your menstrual period. The spasms that release no-longer-needed blood from your uterus are therefore less intense, jarring, and painful. And these contractions don't have to enlist the support of surrounding stomach and back muscles to do their job. Most women who make self-pleasuring a favorite habit find that they experience much less pelvic cramping and greatly diminished or no menstrual backaches. A nice side effect, no?

Reason #15

Self-Pleasuring Enhances Lovemaking with Your Partner.

If you are hot, you can't help but light his fire.

If you have a strong PC muscle to flutter on your lucky man's love organ, and if your body is willing and eager to have lots of deep orgasms, you are going to bring new vigor to his body and sexual imagination.

If you know all your secret erogenous zones and personal turn-ons, you can be much more confident and creative as a lover. You can gently guide him to massage your inner lips counterclockwise, if that's what makes you hot, and let him feel the power of bringing you to a teeth-chattering climax. You can teach him all sorts of sizzling new sex tricks. And if you think your man doesn't really want you to be so brazenly aggressive, think again. According to a book of sex surveys published in 1991, *Do You Do It with the Lights On?*, 91 percent of men—and a whopping 98 percent of men age thirty to fifty-four—not only wanted their partners to take a more active role in sexual play, they wished them to choose the position, place, and procedure.

If you are sexually self-sufficient, you are freer to express this wanton sexuality with your man. That way he doesn't feel so pressured to perform or to puzzle out how to make you fly higher than anybody else has. He doesn't have to spend sleepless nights wondering if he's man enough to make you have the multiple orgasms he's read women secretly expect. You can seductively show him how. Your relaxed self-confidence and euphoria gently rub off on him and magically bring out his natural savage aptitudes and talents.

If you learn how to be deeply intimate with yourself, you can be more intimate with your partner. Likewise, your increased openness encourages him to be more intimate with you. And so that elusive soul sharing that we call intimacy blossoms and grows in your most treasured relationship. A lover once told me, "When you are open with me about your feelings and show me your vulnerable, out-of-control side, I feel I can be open and vulnerable with you. And that makes me feel good."

If you pleasure yourself regularly, you will feel sexier. You will *be* sexier. You will want to make love to your man more often, and you will do so with more gusto and expertise. He will think he has died and gone to heaven.

And last but certainly not least, once you get comfortable with and good at pleasuring yourself, you can put on a really hot, provocative show for your lover. Men *love* to watch women give themselves pleasure. Whether you tie him down and make him watch you for hours or simply wet your finger and slip it quickly inside yourself while staring into his eyes during foreplay, he'll be bewitched.

Every true Sex Goddess has this mouth-watering act in her sexual repertoire. (More details on self-pleasuring for and with your partner in Chapter 10.)

Reason #16

In the Age of HIV, Self-Pleasuring Is the Ultimate in Safe Sex.

Obviously, when you have sex only with yourself, you are in no danger of catching sexually transmitted diseases from someone else. No small concern these days.

But even in partner sex, masturbating with and for each other can be a delightful way to stay safe. Using your hands, vibrators, dildos, and a variety of other sex toys allows you to exchange a lot of loving and fun sexual energy without exchanging any body fluids. And even without body fluids, you can have the sensual moistness of hot sex if you add playful fruit—cucumbers, zucchini, peaches, mushed-up bananas, and so forth—to your repertoire as well. (More details in Chapter 9.)

Reason #17

The Joy of Self-Pleasuring Is Always Available.

Morning, evening, and in-between times, at the office, while traveling, at the beach, on an airplane, when you're bored, when you look or feel too grungy to be seen by another human being, when he's sleeping or watching a football game, between the time he forgets the anniversary of your first kiss and the time when you forgive him, between lovers, after a divorce, when you have the jitters, when you're feeling lonely, when you're feeling sexy and there's no one else around, when you find yourself alone with an X-rated movie or a picture of a man with muscles to die for, whenever wild and crazy thoughts come bouncing unbidden into your head—you can always pleasure yourself and be your own Inner Sex Goddess anytime.

One friend recalls that when she was on her way to see her lover after a three-month separation, she became so excited thinking about his waiting erection that she slipped into an airport bathroom during a stopover, hid herself in a tiny stall, and hastily created her own urgent and explosive, if necessarily silent, orgasm. Thank Goddess, your hands always travel with you!

Reason #18

Self-Pleasuring Is One of the Very Best Ways to Unleash Your Inner Sex Goddess.

Going all the way back to the ancient Sumerian goddess Inanna, divine and human women have innately understood that self-loving is the magical open sesame to the inner realms of power. In fact, Inanna is thought of as the patron goddess of self-pleasuring because she was in a constant state of ecstatic union with herself, and that inner union gave birth to the fertility of all living things. As a matter of fact, self-love *is* the creative state, because when you *know* that you are new each day and that you are a beautiful and perfect temple of pleasure, your benevolent, loving power gives life to all those around you.

Although there are many roads—mental, emotional, and spiritual—to the kingdom of your Inner Sex Goddess, the physical path of sensual awareness and self-pleasuring is usually the most direct route simply because it is so tangible, it is easily accessible, and it fairly bursts with the power of all the five senses. And you will find that if you perform any of what you might consider the mechanical or physically impersonal acts of self-pleasuring with self-*love*, you will evoke the very mental, emotional, and even spiritual feelings of love and affection you usually have only with an intimate mate. Not only is this more fun, stimulating, and satisfying, but it also expands your self-esteem and enhances your ability to communicate love to yourself and your partner—and to receive it from him. And this is what being a true Sex Goddess is all about.

Round her delicate throat

and her silvery breasts

they fastened necklaces of

gold which they,

the gold-filleted Hours,

wear themselves when

they go

to the lovely dances of the

gods in their father's

house.

—First Homeric

"Hymn to Aphrodite,"

translated by Jules

Cashford

4
—
awakening
aphrodite's
body

Even Helen of Troy, a woman so gorgeous and enticing that a war was fought over her, bowed to the awesome beauty and sensual power of Aphrodite, Queen of Heaven and Goddess of the Dawn. Despite one of Aphrodite's temporary disguises as an old woman, Helen recognized the Golden One by the "sweet throat of the goddess and her desirable breasts and her eyes that were full of shining." Most often portrayed nude, the goddess of love was completely unself-conscious about her body and its sexuality, often flaunting it by decorating herself only with golden ornaments. In fact, her unembarrassed naked sensuality and her skill at pleasuring drew countless lovesick men to her like a magnet. Aphrodite was a woman who knew her own erogenous zones and how to activate them to excite herself and her lovers. She truly understood that Woman embodies all the senses in their exalted form and that pleasuring her beautiful body is a natural way for a woman to nourish her erotic soul.

Awakening to the Aphrodite within you, then, means learning how to delight in the pleasures of your own flesh and opening your body to the rich sensations and wanton feelings locked inside. And your own hands, mythically adorned with Aphrodite's brazenly worn gold rings and bracelets, are the keys. So use your golden goddess fingers to love and awaken your body, exploring all its curvy contours, discovering and intensifying its unique pleasure points, and transform it, like Aphrodite's own body, into a sumptuous temple of erotic delights in which you and your man can worship regularly.

It's natural at first to feel some inhibitions about manually pleasing yourself in every wild way you can possibly think of, but try to let those impediments go. Be as bold and as reverent as Aphrodite. If you do feel shy about jumping right in to try *all* of the following suggestions, that's okay. Just start out with what feels comfortable and fun to you. All you may want to do just now is read about them. Don't be surprised, though, if you soon find yourself feeling tempted to try a thing or two, getting more and more adventurous, and even making up your own kinky list of self-pleasuring scenarios. Try to give yourself and your body the benefit of the doubt by crossing over your embarrassment threshold just a little bit. After all, there's no one around to judge you or find out just how much fun you're having. Sip some wine. Relax. Let go. Let your hair down. Brush it out. Like Aphrodite, throw caution, inhibition, and self-consciousness to the wind.

aphrodite's boudoir

It will be much more tempting for your Inner Sex Goddess to come out and play if you create a loving and sensual nest in which she can feel comfortable, safe, and uninhibited. So before you begin your self-play sessions, take the time to create a bedroom Aphrodite would have been proud of. Take the phone off the hook or use the answering machine. Lock the door, post a sign, or do whatever you have to do to ensure privacy. Make sure the room is warm and that you have something to drink. Gather together all the things you might want or need—oils, a towel, a large mirror, a handheld mirror, perfume, wine, sensual foods, music, lingerie, costumes, scarves, sensual fabrics, pillows, erotic literature, sexy pictures, X-rated videos, special erotic objects, vibrators, dildos, and other sex toys of your choice. (More on vibrators and other toys in Chapter 9.) You won't use all of these things every time, but have them handy and gather whichever items you want for that particular session *before* you start. Dress the bed in pretty, fresh linens. Artfully arrange flowers, candles, incense, and evocative paintings or photos. Really focus on creating a special, sensual, and freeing environment for your self-loving ritual. Doing so will make you feel special, sensual, and free.

You can even use your lingerie to add a touch of sass to the interior design of your Aphrodite-like bower. Hang a see-through negligee over the bedpost. Dangle a lacy garter belt from the knob of your dresser. Let several long strings of pearls cascade from one corner of a mirror, and float a silky teddy from the other. Drape lace-topped stockings over a chair. Adorn your pillow with a feather boa and your bedside lamp with a filmy scarf. Display your long satin gloves on the nightstand. Dressing your boudoir in lingerie and jewels will transform it into a sensual palace that beckons your Inner Sex Goddess to appear in its midst—*and* will be a real turn on to your lover.

the breasts beautiful

Aphrodite, like any clever Sex Goddess, certainly knew how to make the most of her feminine assets. So she is depicted, in many statues and paintings, winsomely exposing two of a woman's most naturally glorious and seductive attributes, her breasts. Wildly arousing to most red-blooded men and exquisitely sensitive to your own or a lover's touch, your golden orbs provide a softly feminine place to begin your erotic self-arousal, especially since there is a direct nerve connection between the nipples and the clitoris. Although the intensity of breast and nipple sensation is different for each individual Sex Goddess, Masters and Johnson, the definitive scientific sex researchers, found that about 1 percent of the women they studied were actually capable of going all the way to orgasm simply by caressing their own breasts. But even for the rest of us, breast and nipple massage can provide some highly erotic sensations, and it will usually start your libido sizzling and your divine vaginal nectars flowing.

35. Begin by using the feathery touch of your nails or fingertips to stroke the delicate skin on the side of your torso and under your arms. Slide your fingers down across your stomach and make circles all over your belly and midsection as you raise your hands, and your temperature, up to your swelling breasts. Repeat several times and let yourself float on the hypnotically languorous sensations.

36. Slide your palm in circular motions around the whole area of your breast. Press firmly. Do one breast at a time or use both hands for the two together. Keep this up even after your nipple has become erect. Go faster, slower, harder. Cup as much of each creamy globe in your hand as possible and move them both around. Pull them out. Press them in. Jiggle them. Squeeze them. Imagine that your lover is caressing them. Continue until your breasts feel very warm and tingly.

37. One day, as I leaned over the side of the bed to retrieve the bottle of massage oil I had dropped, I discovered that my breasts felt more sensitive when they were hanging down. I later learned that this is because of increased blood supply to the nipples. So by all means try this leaning-over position. Besides feeling lushly full and tender, your breasts are freer to move as well. Shake them. Give them love taps. Push them together. Massage as in number 36.

38. Massage your nipples. Press on them. Roll them gently between your fingers. Use firmer and firmer pressure. Pinch them. Pull them and hold, or pull and release completely in very rapid strokes. My friend Carrie, a computer specialist with no current lover but plenty of libido, says she likes to hold on to her nipples and shake her breasts with them. Try this for the intensity of the feelings and the visually exciting stimulation.

39. Use one hand to encircle your breast and push it up and out, as a push-up bra would do. This pulls the nipple taut. With your other hand, roll, pinch, and pull the nipple. Wet your fingers and play with it. Rub your fingers back and forth rapidly. Use the pad of your index finger to rotate your nipple in small circles. Flick your fingers or fingernails across each bright berry. Know that your man would be fascinated to watch these maneuvers. Keep all of this up way past the point at which you feel the urge to move to your pubic area.

40. In one very elegant sex movie, I watched with fascination as a woman licked her own nipples. Even though she was rather small-breasted, she was able to accomplish this delightful trick by bringing her breast close to her mouth with her hand, bending her neck down, and using the *bottom* of her tongue to reach the nipple. Close your eyes and feel the lapping of your lover's tongue.

41. Rub your breasts and nipples with silk, velvet, fur, feathers, and even rougher textures like wool, terry cloth, or a very soft brush.

42. Write your partner's name or some sizzling words of love across your chest with your fingertips, spray-on perfume, or hot red lipstick. Use your nipples to dot the *i*'s or make lovely curlicues on appropriate letters.

43. Pull on long, tight leather gloves and play with your breasts and nipples.

44. One friend of mine suggests circling the nipples with an ice cube. She says, "It makes my nipples stand up immediately and feel all wet and fiery." Her husband often requests the pleasure of watching her do this, and he usually jumps right in to lick the watery drips from her up-turned buds. Apparently it makes him "feel all wet and fiery" too.

45. Dab whipped cream or honey on your nipples, or dip them in wine. Lick it off—or let *him* lick it off.

46. Massage your nipples with Vicks VapoRub, Ben-Gay, or some other cream that makes your body heat rise.

47. One day I got the idea from an old photograph of a French courtesan to apply rouge to my nipples. While this is a makeup trick you'll want to secretly expose to your lover, try it on your own, too, and see how ripe and entic-ing your nipples will look. Let the color come off as you massage your pretty rosebuds. Reapply as desired.

48. One bawdy corporate comptroller I know told me that she likes to put her accounting pencils to better use in the privacy of her own boudoir. Pinching her nipples taut, she rubs the rounded pencil erasers, softened from use on her daytime ledgers, against her sensitized areolae.

49. Put on a pretty bra or swimsuit top, but pull the material away so that your nipples and most of your breasts are exposed. Fondle your velvet tips. Now pull the supporting bottom part of the bra up over your breasts so that it rests above the breasts and pushes them down. Again, this puts more pressure into the nipple and sensitizes it. Massage, pull, and pinch your nipples. You can, of course, dress up in any sexy lingerie—camisole, teddy, merry widow, bra with the nipples cut out—and do the same thing. There's no reason you shouldn't look just as gorgeous for yourself as you do for your lover, and besides, your breasts will be sensitized by the extra exquisite pressure. As one young nursing student I know says, "The cool silk and low-cut lace bodice of my favorite camisole do wonderful things with my nipples, especially when I wear it under my uniform."

50. Adorn your fingers with rings before you begin your breast play. Depending on the rings, you may want to turn them around so the showy parts are on the insides of your fingers. They look great, and you can tease your nipples with their different textures as you massage.

51. Use a vibrator on your nipples. Put on one of the ridged or pronged attachments and hold it steady or move it back and forth across the areolae. Circular motions are good, too. My friend Brigitta, a pale Nordic beauty in a still-lusty twenty-year marriage, says she prefers to use a Swedish massager that fits on the back of her hand. She straps it on and lets her vibrating hand and fingers loose on her sensitive breast skin. Sometimes she shares the deli-

cious vibes with her man. (More on vibrators in Chapters 9 and 10.)

52. Get in the bathtub and use your shower massager to wash your nipples with sensation. This is a favorite with several friends of mine, who say it reminds them of being nubile young girls in the shower after gym class, giggling over all the exciting new sensations they were just discovering then. It makes me feel like a Polynesian beauty, standing naked in a steamy tropical waterfall. Discover your own liquid fantasy.

53. Watch yourself in a mirror as you do any or all of the above. Marvel at the hypnotic beauty of your golden orbs, radiating like the Aphrodite within you—to please your own aesthetic senses or titillate your favorite man.

aphrodite's private foreplay

As the Goddess of Love, Aphrodite knew instinctively that the flower of her desire lay resting lightly in her clitoral rosebud and that it had to be treated with the utmost delicacy in order to blossom to its full beauty. While no two buds of love are exactly the same, we modern-day Aphrodites know from all-too-frequent experience that most don't like to be attacked by a too-eager hand. They like to be slowly warmed up first. Hence, your Inner Sex Goddess has gifted you with the instinctive skill of your own brand of private foreplay for the clitoris. Use it for solo as well as partner sex.

While your breast play will already have begun to unfold the petals of your clitoral sensitivity, it's still a good idea to go gently and slowly when approaching direct stimulation of this sensitive area. In fact, some women never touch the glans of their clitoris directly when self-pleasuring; it's just too tender. Instead, they concentrate on the pubic mound. And even though most women do require at least some direct stimulation of the clitoris to have an orgasm, it's still best to start by stimulating the surrounding areas.

54. You might want to begin by stroking your inner thighs and buttocks. Remember to be present in your body, as we learned to do in the body-consciousness exercises in Chapter 2. Really feel all of the luscious sensations you are creating. As you reach the genital area, use a finger or two to gently massage around your anus. (Make sure you are freshly bathed.) Softly rub the perineum (between anus and vulva) with back-and-forth or circular motions.

Give it a few gentle love taps. Concentrate on building a fire in this lower portion of your genitals.

55. Most women enjoy the comforting feeling of cupping their entire pubic mound in one hand. Press and massage gently in circles, from side to side, or back and forth. Knead it like bread. Shake it gently. Recall the feeling of your man's pelvis pumping against this fleshy mound.

56. Still holding your pubis tenderly like a ripe fruit, press your outer vaginal lips together. Then caress them gently up and down so that they begin to open up and expose the moist inner lips. Continue this up-and-down motion, occasionally reaching farther down to include your perineum in one long sensuous stroke over it and your inner lips.

57. You may find it intoxicating to pay some special attention to your delicate perineum. Try sitting with feet flat, knees bent, and legs spread. Rotate your pelvis forward so you can reach it easily. With the touch of a butterfly's wings, caress your inner thighs and allow your fingers to cross over your perineum. Tease this dainty area with your fingernails and inscribe wings, flowers, and stars there. Brush it lightly with a feather or cosmetic brush. Wet your finger and make maddeningly delicious circles. Imagine how provocative this would look to a Peeping Tom.

58. My friend Jenny, a shy librarian with a hot lover who is cleverly disguised as an ordinary mailman, says that when self-pleasuring she loves to vibrate her pubic mound with her whole hand. She suggests laying one finger on each vaginal lip and vibrating them, too. You can use your other hand to vibrate your perineum and/or anus simultaneously if you choose. Jenny admits that she has taught this trick to her favorite mail carrier too.

59. According to Oriental erotic texts, a woman's upper lip is directly connected to her clitoris. While massaging your pubis or vaginal lips, try biting your upper lip, or run the fingernails of your other hand over it, to send tingly signals to the rosebud you're about to touch.

60. If the upper lip connection is not a powerful one for you, try moistening your lips with Vaseline or a lovely supermoist lip gel. Lightly rub your fingers over your glistening lips. Slip a finger between them.

61. Recline languorously on a pillow and let your legs fall open. Rest the palm of your hand on your pubic area but without touching your clitoris. Exerting a firm but light pressure, use your hand to move the skin of your pubis around in slow circles over the underlying tissue and bone. Occasionally release your hand and lightly pat your beautiful mound of pleasure. Alternate light patting with deep circling until moans escape your lips. After observing their women get all hot and bothered by doing this, men seem to feel especially clever when they "invent" this foreplay technique to use on you themselves. So be sure to let your lover catch you at it.

62. While holding your vaginal area, move your hips around in circles. Undulate like a snake. Or do some pelvic thrusts à la Elvis. Keep your hand loose enough so that your pelvic motions cause it to slide lightly around your moving mound. I have a very modest friend who claims that pretending she's a rock star and flagrantly thrusting her hips around frees her wilder, lustier self to come out of hiding. So, with her hand suggestively placed over her naked sex, this is how she begins every self-pleasuring session. When you try this, you may want to imagine that you are getting private lessons in hip swiveling from the King himself.

the ripe rosebud

The lovely little organ whose only function is to give pleasure originally got its name from Aphrodite's compatriots, the ancient Greeks. Wise in the ways of both loving and philosophy, they understood that this tiny knob was the key to a woman's orgasmic pleasure. So from their word for "key," *kleis*, they coined the term *kleitoris*. Just as every door key is different from all others, every woman's clitoris looks and behaves differently and has highly individual preferences for stimulation. These preferences can range from no direct touch at all to indirect pressure with only the palm of the hand to intense and deep finger massage directly on the glans. So there is no "right" way to pleasure your ripe rosebud. There is only the way that feels good, comfortable, and sensuous to you. And that may change from day to day or from month to month, depending on your emotional state, your physical condition, and your monthly cycle. So consult your Inner Sex Goddess and be adventurous yet sensitive to the responses of your own body. Here are some suggestions to try out as you take the time to deepen the sensual bond between you and your own pleasure organ.

63 . Lubrication is not only the key to a good relationship with your clitoris, but it also extends the sensations over larger parts of your vaginal area. So before you caress this delicate bud directly, make sure your fingers are moistened with your own saliva, the juices from your vagina, K-Y jelly, or oil. You can use baby oil, coconut oil, vegetable oil, or a good massage oil. Olive oil is probably a little too thick, but sunflower, safflower, and grapeseed are good choices. Scented massage oils add another dimension

of sensuality; the flower essences, musk, and ylang-ylang are particularly potent for sexual play. Just make sure the oil you use contains no alcohol, which can irritate the delicate mucous membranes. And avoid Vaseline too; because it's not water soluble it can be uncomfortable and unhealthy if it gets in your vagina or urethra.

Experiment with different lubes for different occasions. Your own juices are always available, completely natural, and very earthy and sexy. Oils, which are slipperier, are good for intense friction and hand gliding. Scented oils add luscious aromatic vapors and can catalyze some exotic fantasies. The choice is deliciously yours.

64. You may want to begin by using your entire hand—heel, palm, and fingers closed together. Cup your hand over your pubic mound, touching your clitoris lightly, and inscribe circles around and over it. Press with the palm or heel of your hand. Then try using your overhanging fingers. Keep the circular motions going as you explore the sensations arising from varying pressures and parts of the hand. Most women find that sustained repetitive movements are the most satisfying. Also lovely is imagining that your lover's hand or penis is caressing you tenderly there.

65. Karol, a sexy secretary I know, says she likes to rub her clitoris indirectly through its shaft. You can stroke

on the right side if you are right-handed and on the left if you are left-handed. Switch sides when you feel the urge; this technique can provide an entirely different sensation, and it can renew sensitivity when one side gets "tired."

66. Experiment with various kinds of touch and rhythms—light feathery pats, gentle massage, firm steady pressure, intense rubbing, playful love slaps, fast circles, slow back-and-forth movements, languid strokes alternating with quick taps, rolling motions, pinches, vibrating with your hands or fingers. When you find a touch that really lights your fire that day, stay with it for a while. As you explore your own key rhythms and touches, sense the wetness seeping into your loins.

67. If you can stand it, try massaging your rosebud firmly with just one finger. Play around with circling, side-to-side, and rolling motions. Create a vibrating motion with your finger as you press down hard. Rock your pelvis up to meet your trembling digit as you would to reach for a lover's touch. Add another finger and probe some more. If the pleasure gets too agonizingly intense, stop momentarily and massage your thighs or belly instead.

68. Like my friend Bess, a forty-something banker, you might like to try taking hold of the shaft of your clitoris with thumb and forefinger. Roll it between the fingers.

Pull on it. Move it up and down. Squeeze. Release. Roll it again. Try using two different fingers, or the fingers of your two hands. Bess says, "I need a lot of stimulation, and somehow this direct, forceful handling really gets my body humming."

69. Contract your PC muscles rhythmically while caressing your clitoris. Squeeze and release the muscles around your anus. These tightening movements heighten the sensitivity of your clitoral nerves. Let your contractions roll back and forth between the two areas as you continue rubbing your love button. Test varying rhythms. Do it to rock music.

70. I always wondered why the women in X-rated movies frequently use both hands to stretch their outer lips wide before provocatively stroking themselves. Often we think that their immodest actions are meant only to provide better sight lines or are done purely for the benefit of some debauched man. But I've found that, as usual, women are much smarter than that. After all, men don't invent these unusual and creative moves. Women do. Because, yes, they drive men crazy, but more important, they feel great. Through personal experimentation, I've learned that spreading your love lips open the way these women do makes the sensitive skin of your clitoris feel deliciously exposed and taut. Try it yourself, and then stimulate your lovely pleasure organ any way you choose. Imagine that *you* are a raunchy porn star—and your man is salivating over every frame of the movie.

71. A luscious thing to do while gloriously outspread is to thump your clitoris lightly and quickly with your middle finger or the side of your hand. (Wouldn't a slap from your lover's penis be lovely too!) Alternate with hard circular massaging.

72. Sara, a dietitian with six kids, says that whenever she can steal a moment to herself, one of her favorite techniques is to stroke down toward her clit from the top of her pubic mound, not quite touching its surface or sometimes gliding lightly over the top of it. Adapting a technique she learned from her deliciously randy husband, she occasionally slides her fingers down farther to gather some juice from her vagina and then circles her wet fingertips around her sensitized bud. Try it. You'll like it too.

73. You can learn a lot from watching a man play with himself. Because the clitoris is closely akin to the penis, you can adapt almost any male masturbation method to the caressing of your love bud. For instance, try holding and stroking your clitoris up and down as he would his penis. Or slide from bottom to tip with the fingers of one hand, and then switch to the other hand. Do

this quickly and with upstrokes only. Improvise with anything that works for him.

74. While caressing your clitoris, squeeze or rub your vaginal lips. Using only one hand will keep the rhythms and movements in concert, but you could also try using two hands to circle clockwise with one while the other moves counterclockwise. Or one hand could administer gentle blows while the other presses and massages deeply.

75. Pull gently on your pubic hair while teasing your clitoris. For me, this always brings back arousing memories of a wonderful man who loved to reach around in front of me and hold my pubic hair while he rubbed his penis against my clitoris from behind.

76. Tug on a nipple in rhythm with your clitoral strokes. Roll both between your fingers. Massage in tandem circles as your legs fall invitingly open for an imaginary lover.

77. In one sex class I attended, the instructor asserted that "any good clitoral massage should include the urethra which is actually part of the G-spot and is therefore highly sensitive to erotic pleasuring." At the next class most of the women, including me, excitedly attested to the truth of this theory. In the name of scientific research, test it out for yourself.

78. Tickle the underside of your love bud with one finger while stroking, patting, rubbing, or flicking the side or top of the clitoral hood with another. This intensely erotic trick can make you climb the walls, so apply it judiciously.

79. As you lovingly stroke your clitoris, be aware of how the sensations change. At the beginning it will be tender and want a light touch. But as your excitement grows and you get closer to orgasm, your rosebud will swell and become harder and stiffer, much as a man's penis does. At this point, press harder, circle or stroke faster, vibrate more intensely. Thrust your pelvis against your hand. Arch your back and pant, moan, or scream.

80. My friend Rosie reminds me of a plum—small, round, and sweet, but tart at the same time. Very frank about the fact that she's been self-pleasuring regularly since the age of five, she says, "I love to massage my soft spot [the perineum, between the vagina and anus] with the fingertips of both hands. Then I smooth my fingers up between my vaginal lips, collecting some wetness so my fingers can slide more easily, then I let them slide over my clit, down outside the outer lips, and back to my soft spot. Each

time I reach my clit, I give it a little extra push, squeeze, or roll. After about three minutes of this, I'm really shaking. But then I circle my clit and soft spot with both hands at the same time, which makes me feel unbearably sexy, until I have an orgasm that vibrates my whole body."

81. While you rub your pleasure organ, try bearing down as you do when you have a bowel movement. This pushes the entire pelvic floor down and brings more pressure into the clitoris, making it exquisitely sensitive and trembly. Many women report that this action alone can bring on an orgasm very quickly.

82. Don some of your laciest, sexiest panties and massage your clitoris through them. Pull the two sides together at the crotch so that you have a thin, taut ribbon of fabric to pull against your pulsing love bud. Since this is as exciting to feel as it is to watch in the mirror, keep it in mind for a visual turn-on when you're in bed with your man.

83. A technique I modified from an Oriental love text is really meant for pleasuring a man's "Jade Stalk." But there's no reason your "Rosy Stem" shouldn't enjoy it too. Hold your little stem between your fingers and stroke it in rhythm to the throbbing of your heart. Then give it one fast up-and-down stroke, and return to the slow, sensuous

stroking for about ten seconds. Then two rapid up-and-down strokes and back to the slow stuff for another ten seconds. Increase to three fast, and back to slow, and so on.

84. After your love button has become engorged with excitement, try holding it between your fingers while you use the palm of your other hand, or your flattened fingers, to massage lightly in circles over the tip. Fantasize, if you wish, that it's really the pulsing head of your man's penis that's rubbing you there.

the voluptuous vagina

Aphrodite wasn't the only one who was hip to the benefits of loving her own body. Since ancient times, Taoist medical practitioners and Tantric initiates have taught that to have a whole and healthy body and mind, you must fully love your genitals and the sexual energy harbored there. When you come to know and love your vagina as the mysterious cavelike home of the sacred life force, you will find yourself developing a new, more charismatic relationship with your femininity, your sexuality, and your man.

While some women prefer to explore the voluptuousness of their vaginas first before moving on to the clitoris —

feeling that the dainty bud is just too sensitive in the beginning — others feel that starting with clitoral massage warms up the vagina's fewer nerve endings so that it becomes more eager for erotic touch. But whatever your personal preference, it's delicious to pleasure both erogenous zones at the same time. You can practice the following techniques while you are massaging your pearly bud or try them all by themselves. Mix and match to your libido's content.

85. Stroke and massage all around your vaginal opening. Run your finger up and down over the juicy slit, gently opening it wider and wider. Pull the lips apart and caress the moist skin just inside the opening. Many women find that the wider their vaginal opening is stretched, the more acute the sensations. Relish this feeling of vulnerable exposure.

86. Dip one or two fingers into your voluptuously wet furrow. In addition to keeping your fingers lubricated for clitoral stroking, this adds another level of sensation. (Short fingernails are a prerequisite.) Press upward to feel the back of your clitoral membrane and explore its moist sensitivities from this other side. If you curl your hand, you can keep the knuckles of your free fingers pressed against the outside of your clitoris at the same time.

87. Slide one or more fingers in and out of your vagina just as you like your lover's penis to do. Slant your hand and sweep your fingers around to feel the luscious friction from all angles and against all surfaces of your vaginal canal. Stretch your lips wide. Go fast. Go slow. Tease yourself unmercifully.

88. A very sultry woman I know says she likes to insert just one finger about two inches deep. Then she crooks her finger and tickles first the upper and then the lower walls of her vaginal barrel. It's "exquisite torture," says she.

89. While performing 87 and 88, use the thumb of the same hand to rub your clitoris or pull on your inner lips. This is much like the tug of your lover's penis as it dips in and out between all those sensitive tissues.

90. Adapting a cooking technique for stuffing chickens, I discovered that it feels heavenly to slip your thumb inside your vagina and then glide it in circular motions against your other fingers, massaging the thin, wet membrane of your vaginal wall between them. Try out your own inner recipe.

91. When your vaginal tissues are engorged with sexual juices and excitement, their sensitivity to touch and

pressure is magnified. One inch of thumb can feel like nine inches of a man. So if you simply anchor your thumb tip inside and press it down toward your spine, you can mobilize your fingers to simultaneously tease your clitoris with circular massage or up-and-down sweeps.

92. Plunge into the depths of your coral abyss with two or three fingers and rotate them as if you were stirring up a scrumptious batter. Or spread your fingers out like a scissors, as far apart as you can. Open and release several times.

93. Adorn your index finger with a big flashy ring and thrust it in and out of your steamy vagina. The X-rated movie stars who love to perform this act for the camera know that it adds elegant beauty to the scene and feels fantastic, too. Show this one to your lover.

94. Experiment with different body positions. Kneel, lie on your stomach, stand in front of a mirror. Or try lying on your back with feet braced against the headboard or wall. This, and kneeling with your legs spread, tenses the pelvic muscles and pulls your vagina taut to heighten sensation.

95. When her husband is away, my friend Karen says she uses one of those standing pillows with arm rests

as a substitute. She snuggles into its "embrace" or props herself against her stand-in hubby's open "legs" while she diddles herself just the way he would.

96. With the flat of your hand, try stretching the soft skin of your pubic mound upward toward your belly. Hold it taut while you slide the fingers of your other hand quickly in and out of your tightened opening. Conjure up your favorite fantasy.

97. Spread open your outer lips and use your thumb to gently strum the inner ones. Play this tune for your man and his drum major's baton.

98. My friend Gail, a brilliant graphic artist with fiery red hair and tons of freckles and boyfriends, graciously offered to share one of her favorite maneuvers. She says she loves to insert two fingers into her vagina and press her clitoris with two fingers of the other hand. Then she rubs the two sets of fingers together through all the sensitive skin between. I've found you can also do this with only one hand by inserting your middle finger and using your thumb for the clitoris. What a divine massage!

99. Hold open your vaginal lips with the fingertips of both hands. Knead the flower-petal skin in circular motions, down toward the anus, around toward the inner

thighs, and up toward the clitoris. Keep going around and around till you can't stand it anymore.

100. When a Hawaiian friend of mine mentioned that she likes to go "swimming with the dolphins" when she pleasures herself, I couldn't wait to hear the details. She says she lays her hand flat against the entire vaginal area. Then she lets the tip of her middle finger tease her vaginal opening and occasionally slide in and out. She alternates pressing hard against the top and undersides of her pubic mound with the heel and ball of her palm. Then she rolls and undulates her whole hand in wavelike movements, the way dolphins swim. Or you can let your middle finger lie against your clitoris with the fingertip just inside your vagina; then circle, roll, and undulate your hand like a sinuous creature of the deep.

101. While thrusting your fingers in and out like a lover's hard shaft, massage your inner thighs, belly, derriere, or nipples with your other hand. All of these sensitive tissues are erotically connected and will respond quite intensely to tender caresses at any location. You rarely get to experience these delightful combinations with a partner because it's just too awkward; so take the opportunity to treat yourself to this extra loving.

the love muscle

The PC muscle, the one you squeeze to stop the flow of urine, is one of the greatest love secrets in Aphrodite's body. Just by twitching it, any ordinary goddess can give and receive ambrosial delights worthy of the heights of Mount Olympus. A well-toned PC muscle will greatly enhance your pleasure during self-loving as well as while making love with a partner, and it will drive most men wild when flexed against their penis. When strong and healthy, this muscle is highly sensitive to vaginal stimulation and is actually able to bring his thrusting penis closer to your G-spot. It makes for increased lubrication, stronger clitoral sensations, more intense and more frequent climaxes, and even multiple orgasms. How does all this magic take place?

Lying about one inch below the surface of the skin, the PC muscle runs from the pubic bone to the tailbone, firmly supporting the anus and internal sex organs. It may be as thin as half an inch or as thick as two inches. In addition to cradling your organs of pleasure, the love muscle is also home to the pudendal nerve, which detects feeling around the clitoris, the vaginal lips and opening, and the anus. This nerve sends signals to the brain that say "This feels good; send blood and energy here," and it later receives brain signals that start the pleasurable contractions of orgasm. After every contraction of your PC muscle, whether you flex it deliberately or an orgasm does it for you, blood rushes into the vagina, making the tissue swell and darken and increasing lubrication. Some women describe this sensation as a melting or "I love you" feeling. In fact, besides the actual nerve connections between the PC muscle and the brain, there seems to be some extrasensory bond between the love muscle and the heart that, when activated, makes you feel soft, fuzzy, and warm inside.

The miraculous abilities and pleasures of a well-trained PC muscle are extolled in the ancient love texts of the Oriental and Tantric traditions, too. They describe women with such a high degree of PC control that they were able to pick up small objects and thrust them out with great force, using only their vaginal muscles. Imagine what they could have done with a man's penis! But the real beauty of such dexterity is that they were able to provide their own intense vaginal and clitoral stimulation — without a penis, dildo, vibrator, pillow, hand, or finger. Their agile vaginas were completely self-contained pleasure units. We too can share in this special female magic simply by exercising our PC muscles regularly. And you will find that these sexual calisthenics are a major turn-on in and of themselves.

102. The fastest and easiest way to get started enjoying your PC muscle is to simply flex it quickly about twenty-five times—anytime, anywhere; no one will know. The sensation will be more intense if you put your attention on your clitoris or vaginal opening while you are squeezing. This will strongly focus your awareness, energy, and excitement. In fact, some women say they can reach a climax from this exercise alone. At the very least, it will bring your Inner Sex Goddess immediately to attention.

103. When your muscles have something to resist their squeezing pressure, they can develop even faster, and you can get a better idea of just how strongly you are flexing. Insert a finger, a clean carrot, or a dildo into your vagina, squeeze and hold it for five seconds. Release and squeeze again. After several of these, do some quick clenches. Swoosh the inserted object around to provide differing levels of pressure and to excite your PC muscle into more intense flexing. See what it feels like to push the muscles *out* as well; you can accomplish this by pressing down as you do when you have a bowel movement. If you close your eyes and focus on your moist vaginal walls sliding against the object, you will find a warm, pleasurable sensation building up inside you. Let your libido and your Inner Sex Goddess take it from there.

$104.$ Here's a Tantric PC exercise that always makes me feel like a volcano boiling, oozing, and erupting. You may want to perform this one to music, as I do. Stand with your feet apart at shoulder width and begin slowly squeezing your PC muscle. Breathe in deeply with each squeeze, and exhale with each release. Feel the volcanic heat coming up the insides of your thighs and into your womb. Keeping your feet firmly planted, rock your hips back and forth sensuously—rock forward as you inhale and squeeze, rock back as you exhale and release. Feel the heat building in your loins. After a bit, move your hips around in circles as you continue flexing and releasing. Imagine that you are a hula dancer or a belly dancer; sway your pelvis provocatively and perform expertly sexual internal dances. Feel the volcanic heat radiating from your pelvis as you release a low "ahhh" with each exhalation and PC relaxation. As you continue undulating your hips and flexing your love muscle, imagine that the hot energy you are generating rises up through your belly, breast, throat, and face to the top of your head, where it showers you with tingly liquid ecstasy. Slowly return to earth whenever you're ready.

$105.$ The ancient Chinese Taoists developed a complex set of stone egg exercises designed to strengthen and tone the vaginal muscles. For a time, these exercises were taught only to the Empress and the Emperor's concubines in the royal palace, supposedly so they could better please the Emperor. And I'm sure they did. But these wise women knew that they were secretly enjoying themselves, enhancing their health, and even prolonging their youth. If, like these multitalented royal ladies, you'd like to increase your sexual energy and expertise, here's a simplified version of the egg techniques.

Select a stone or a wooden egg about one inch in diameter from a gem store or a New Age shop. Keep it scrupulously clean with soap and water. Always perform the egg exercises while standing, feet apart at shoulder width, and warm yourself up first with some self-massage. Insert the egg into your vagina, large end first, using your own juices or some oil to lubricate it. Hold the egg inside you by clenching the muscles at the opening of your vagina. When you first start practicing, simply feel your internal muscles contracting against the smooth egg. Get used to holding it inside you and feeling how it moves.

As you become more expert, you can move on to more advanced techniques such as the following. Inhale as you squeeze the muscles at the other end of your vagina, deep inside. Then begin to move the egg up and down, and from side to side, with the muscles in the middle section of your vagina. This takes practice and dexterity, but the sense of passionate control you will experience is worth the effort. Even if you just learn to keep the egg snug inside, you can't help but revel in its smooth sensuality and the delicious feeling of fullness it provides. Try different size eggs, too—bigger egg, more fullness; smaller egg, more exercise and control. Eventually you can train your vaginal muscles to draw the egg in all by themselves and expel it forcefully. Your vaginal expertise, whether applied to an egg, a finger, or a penis, is limited only by your imagination.

the bewitching behind

Aphrodite Kallipygos (Aphrodite of the Lovely Backside) captivated scores of lovers simply by undraping her fleshy fanny. She truly understood that a woman's behind has the power to ignite her own inner fires as well as to bewitch almost any man. You'll begin to understand the fanny's electric power if you use your erotic imagination to recall how delicious it feels when you rub yours up against your man's body while lying in the spoon position, or when he cups your luscious cheeks in his hands as you make love. I didn't really catch on to this myself until about the twentieth time my lover, plunging into me from behind, moaned in the throes of ecstasy, "Your ass looks so fine when it quivers, and it feels so good bouncing up against me." Meanwhile I actually *was* quivering, with even more intense pleasure than he! So complete the awakening of your Aphrodite's body by discovering, with your own gentle hands and fingers, the unexpected pleasures of derriere and anal massage, a sensual treat fit for a goddess.

106. While you are pleasuring your vagina or your clitoris, smooth your hands over the silky curves of your behind. Use feathery fingertips or firm palm pressure; squeeze gently or hard; scrape your nails across the delicate skin; it's especially sensitive because it is rarely exposed to sun and air. Rub the rough lace or cool silk of a camisole against your fanny. Don your elbow-length gloves or furry mittens and massage your rounded curves and the deep valley between them. Experiment with wet hands, ringed fingers, naked knuckles, and rolling forearms. Have fun with feathers.

107. Diane, an otherwise very buttoned-down attorney friend of mine, says she likes to rub her behind against the cool sheets of her bed the whole time she is pleasuring herself in other ways. Sometimes she places a pillow between derriere and bed to add a new sensation and a higher elevation. Or she lays her backside against the rough wool of the blanket and undulates with the motions of her vaginal self-play. Occasionally she even stands with her back against the wall—she has textured wallpaper, but even smooth paint will do—and slides up and down while she uses her hands to caress the front of her body. She loves to find different textures to stimulate her bottom during self-play and often sits in various locations to produce interesting new effects—smooth, hard wooden chairs; rocking chairs; plump velvet couches; canvas deck chairs; rope hammocks; fabric-covered office chairs that roll around; desks; kitchen countertops; toilet seats; bathtubs, dry or with a thin layer of water; rugs and carpets; stairs; grass; sand; the rough bark of a tree limb; a swing; a large basket—the possibilities are truly limitless.

108. The anus is one of the most erotically sensitive spots on your body, and if you are freshly bathed, it's just as clean as the rest of you. So don't be squeamish about discovering its pleasures. Just remember that the secret to enjoying anal play is lubrication—either your own saliva or a good massage oil. Start out by simply wetting your index finger and pressing or massaging all around and over the outside of the opening. Keep your mind and body focused on the erotic by simultaneously massaging your nipples, clitoris, or vagina. As you enjoy these luscious sensations, let yourself relax and feel good about this often outcast part of your body. Indulge in ecstatic sense memories of your lover's tickling caresses to your behind. Breathe deeply and consciously relax your sphincter muscles. Then gently and slowly work your finger inside your anus and keep massaging. Circular or come-hither motions are best at first; save the in-and-out movements for later when you're more accustomed to the feeling and more

relaxed. Discover your personal internal hot spots by trying different pressures, motions, and locations. Many women find an especially delicious place to rub is on the vagina side of the anal canal, which is really the other side of the magical G-spot. In fact, this is how many otherwise nonorgasmic women finally achieve a shuddering climax. But even as a simple accompaniment to the main melody of clitoral or vaginal self-pleasuring, anal massage is a delight you won't want to miss.

109. An especially deep and earthy feeling of ecstasy can be achieved by massaging—from both sides—that thin, silken spot that lies inside between the vaginal and anal canals. You can do this by inserting the finger of one hand in the vulva and the finger of the other hand into the anus, then rubbing them together. It's probably easiest to accomplish this while lying on your back with legs drawn up to your chest. One inventive friend of mine says she likes to leave a hand free for breast or clitoral massage at the same time. So she simply uses her thumb inside the vagina and slides the pinky of the same hand into her anal opening, bringing thumb and pinky together around the delicate internal tissues. Considering the possibilities for variation here, discovering your own style of anal play—and later revealing them to your panting lover—can be at least half the fun.

*Woman is the creator of
the universe, the universe
is her form. . . .
Whatever form she takes,
whether the form of a
man or a woman, is the
superior form. In woman
is the form of all things,
of all that lives and moves
in the world. There is no
jewel rarer than woman,
no condition superior to
that of a woman.*

—Saktisangama Tantra

5

---

the mirror

of sensual

transfor-

mation

Priestesses of the Tantric tradition, sometimes called yoginis, took great pride in the firepower of their bodies and sexuality to burn up obsolete ideas and beliefs, transforming them into jewels of expanded sensual perception and wisdom. Intimately familiar with the physical and esoteric function of every part of their bodies, they deliberately adopted certain postures and palpated special body points that enhanced their sensual energy flow. They had the ability to see the true nature of their resplendent physical forms reflected in a quiet pool, a looking glass, or a lover's eyes.

By looking into the yogini's Mirror of Sensual Transformation and seeing yourself as a magnificent creature made for love, you too will be able to shed worn-out ideas about puffy tummies and sagging chins, throw radiant light on heretofore hidden and mysterious places, and come to truly understand that "in woman is the form of all things." If you approach this anatomical exploration as an exhilarating journey of rediscovery, you will no doubt have provocative revelations about yourself and your sexuality—revelations that will make you an unusually creative bed partner. In fact, sensuality experts as diverse as ancient Tantrics and modern-day sex therapists *require* expertise in this kind of self-pleasuring investigation before moving on to any other kind of sexual teachings. It's an eye-opening fount of knowledge and an autoerotic turn-on. So grab your Inner Sex Goddess, light a few candles, and make a special ritual out of discovering the divine firepower of your own sumptuous body.

110. Set up a full-length mirror and a good-sized hand mirror in a private, quiet room. Lock the door and make sure you will have at least an hour and a half completely to yourself. Then start out by creating a soft sensual mood—after all, you are about to seduce the sacred inner you. Take a scented bath. Light some candles and incense. Put on sultry music. Fix your hair in a pretty style and dab on some musky perfume or body lotion. Don your sexiest lingerie and pose before the mirror, proudly erect with hands on hips, as the yoginis do, or reclining provocatively like the centerfold models in *Playboy* magazine. Then seductively strip down to complete nakedness, or perhaps leave on a string of pearls or a thin chain around your waist, or a flower in your hair. Think of all this as preparation for your lover. Just as Cleopatra's attendants would have readied her for romance with scented milk baths and opulent adornments, so should you carefully prepare for a loving session with yourself. Crawl into the translucent, hot skin of your Inner Sex Goddess and enjoy.

Then sit or stand about ten inches away from the full-length mirror and stare gently into your eyes. Relax, breathe deeply, and imagine your eyes becoming like soft jelly. Look into your soul. The Tantrics recommend eye-gazing like this for about five to ten minutes, longer if you can. Really let yourself trespass on the inner you—sultry, deeply sensual, romantic, tender, and loving.

Begin to explore your body with your hands. Look at yourself from all angles—front, back, side, standing, kneeling, sitting with legs apart and together. Do not criticize. If you have to, imagine that you are from another planet where lumpy thighs are considered exquisitely sexual. Examine every nook and cranny with the handheld mirror, praising and patting each delicious body part. Many women find that looking at their own bodies this way turns them on. Admire and caress your entire body, except the genitals, for at least forty-five minutes.

Now lovingly examine your pubic area in both the full-length and handheld mirrors. If you have a makeup mirror with a magnifying side, use that, too. Observe the different colors, shapes, and textures. Label each part by touching it gently. Notice first the contour of your upper pubis. Does it slope invitingly down to your vulva, or is it a high, provocative mound? Is your pubic hair a dark, thick bush or more like wispy blond grass? Does it form a triangle? a bold band? a small circlet peeping over the edge? How would someone who was mesmerized by it, like an adoring lover, describe this part of you?

As you slide your fingers farther down and along the hair-covered outer lips of your vulva (labia majora), be aware of their spongy or pillowy texture. See if yours are puffy, flat, long, or curved. Would you describe their color as burnt sienna? dusky rose? amorous amber? Regarded by some as the female equivalent of a man's scrotum, these lips contain glands that, when aroused, release a film of sweat that chemically stimulates and attracts the opposite sex. Did you know they were so enticing?

When you stroke your hairless inner lips (labia minora), notice their smooth, moist slickness. They too contain glands that produce lubricating juices. Feel, smell, and even taste these fluids when they arrive. Try to characterize the size, shape, and texture of your inner lips, which vary greatly from woman to woman. Some women have described theirs as having "the feel of satin sheets," "caviar coloring," "edges like a doily," or "the clean lines of a Jaguar racing car." Do yours remind you of a flower? the inside of a peach? folded velvet? a sea creature? a fleshy heart? a yin-yang symbol? Is the left lip bigger or smaller than the right one? Do the inner lips stay tucked demurely inside the outer ones, or do they protrude or droop temptingly? Notice how the texture, moisture, and warmth of both your inner and outer lips change as you excite them, engorging with blood, thickening, and darkening.

Then slide on up to the clitoris, or the Jewel Terrace, as it's lovingly known in the Orient. Slip back the hood of skin that covers it and run your finger along the shaft. Although it is much like a man's penis, the clever little clitoris is unique—no organ whose *sole* function is to stimulate and elevate erotic pleasure exists on a man's body. The most sensitive of your sexual organs, it is often the *key* (remember that's the literal translation of "clitoris" in Greek) to sensual ecstasy. That's because it is crammed full of tender nerve endings, more than any other part of the vulva. Here too are intensely sensitive microscopic fibers called Pacinian corpuscles, jammed even closer together in the tip of the clitoris, making this apex a keenly acute receptor of sharp pleasure—or pain, if too roughly handled. Gently experiment with differing strokes and amounts of pressure on your clitoris, touching it directly—with a wet finger is usually best—and indirectly through the surrounding tissues, up and down the shaft, across the tip, circling the whole area. How does it look and feel as it receives these different types of loving attention?

Usually about 3/4 inch to 1 1/4 inches long, each woman's clitoris will have a size, shape, and character all its own. Some women have described theirs as a "tiny dewdrop," a "tight, pulsing rosebud," or a "big flashy cultured pearl." How would you describe your "love diamond"? In an Aboriginal creation myth, the two Djanggawo sisters had clitorises so long that they formed grooves on the earth as they walked, and the well-endowed sisters had to rest their clitorises on their thighs in order to have access to their vaginas. What is the relationship of your clitoris to the vaginal opening? Is it a mere finger's width away, or more like a wrist's width distant? It may be that women whose clitorises are very near to their vaginas are the ones able to have orgasms through intercourse alone.

As you press and massage your love bud, notice the tiny ridge of tissue that runs underneath. Not just the little pebble you see on the outside, the clitoris is actually a much larger organ that lies partially buried beneath the surface. In actuality, the clitoral system is at least 30 percent larger inside your body than it is on the outside, so you can experience flashes of burning pleasure when it is stimulated from inside your vagina too. The clitoral shaft is composed of two rods of spongy tissue that fill with blood during sexual arousal. (It should be enlarging and becoming more sensitive and "erect" right now as you touch it.) These two rods bend backward and connect with the pelvic bones on either side of the vagina, while another muscular rod extends from the inner part of the shaft, splits in two, and surrounds the vaginal opening. During arousal, these muscles contract and keep blood from leaving the clitoris, helping to keep it enlarged and tugging gently on it as well. Try stroking your vaginal lips as you watch in the mirror what happens when the pressure on these connected tissues sends thrilling messages to your clitoral bud. Imagine that your lover's penis, rubbing anywhere in the vicinity, will do the same.

As you massage your inner lips, notice how your vagina naturally opens to your finger. Approach this portal in a sacred way, as do the people of the Sepik River in New Guinea. They enter and exit their ceremonial houses by crawling between the outspread legs of carved figures of the sacred feminine form. Slip through the entrance of your inner cave to feel the creamy warmth within, and the differences in texture and sensation between all the sides of its elastic walls. Some sexologists assert that the first third of the vagina is more sensitive to touch than the remainder because more nerve endings are located there, and that the deeper two-thirds is more responsive to pressure and stretching. Many women feel differently. Slide your fingers deep inside and see what's true for you.

Feel the power of your PC muscles as you alternately squeeze and push them against your fingers. Watch your muscles contract in the mirror. Imagine how this milking action would feel to a penis. Explore the thick folds of your vaginal walls, some running horizontally and some vertically, and the milky secretions they produce. Feel, smell, and taste this love juice.

Delight in your vagina's miraculous ability to compress or expand to accommodate the smallest tampon, the largest erect penis, and even the birth of a baby. See if you can get your fingers far enough inside to feel the way the upper two-thirds of your vagina opens up like a sultan's tent, and the lower third swells to create a warm, spongy, soft area of tissue that will eventually grip a penis tightly. Experience the particular way your magical inner cave lifts and opens wide as you become more aroused, pulling your vaginal lips apart, sensitizing and flooding them, too, with blood and moisture.

In the Quodoushka tradition, a Cherokee equivalent of Tantra, the depth of the vagina and its characteristics are thought to be important clues to a woman's entire sexual temperament. In Harley Swiftdeer's *Quodoushka Manual*, five female genital anatomy types are described, including Dancing Woman and Sheep Woman. With a vagina of average depth, small inner lips, and a high, small clitoris that springs up from beneath its hood like a dancer, Dancing Woman prefers a lover with a short, thin penis (*tipili*, or "sacred snake"). Sheep Woman, on the other hand, has a deeper vagina, larger, thicker vulval lips, and a lower, more hidden clitoris. She produces copious lubrication and can climax only if she feels a heart connection to her partner. What is the nature of your "feathered flying serpent" *(tupuli)*, as the Cherokees call it?

Look in the mirror now to see how gorgeous your vulva appears when excited with love, and how much it has changed since you started this scintillating adventure. Reconsider your vagina not as an unattractive and unknown void but as a divine portal to the most secret parts of the inner you, a doorway to your Inner Sex Goddess, a Vermilion Gate, as the Orientals call it, through which to receive your lover in the most royal fashion. Praise and perfume this wondrous, sacred part of yourself.

Since there are few things more beautiful than a woman aroused, gaze in the mirror now and see how gorgeous your whole body is—how pink your luscious lips have become, how your eyes have dilated and your skin flushed. Admire the way your breasts have swollen and your nipples have become harder and darker, erect with desire. Your clitoris, too, is erect and pulsating. Your vaginal lips may have swollen up to three times their normal size, and they may have darkened to a deep wine or a bright red. Your toes, feet, or stomach muscles may be fluttering or quivering in a high state of turbulent excitation. Notice how your body not only *looks* different but also *smells* and *moves* differently. Take in the whole image of you in full bloom—glorious, sensual, and powerful. Tell your reflection how radiant, delicate, sexy, graceful, glowing, shapely, and devastating you look. Bask in your beauty and thank yourself, your body, and your Inner Sex Goddess for revealing their wonderful secrets to you.

| | | . Finish off this mirrored self-play by continuing to arouse and ravish yourself almost to the point of orgasm—at least three times and maybe up to fifteen times. With each buildup to and retreat from the point of no return, your excitement will reach higher and higher levels. Then finally let yourself climax, watching your orgasm

in the mirror, and float in the dreamy sensations for an eternity.

112. A very saucy friend of mine, who actually appeared in a *Playboy* video of over-forty-and-still-fabulous women, suggests the following alternative way to discover your own body: perform all of the activities in this chapter not in front of a mirror but before a video camera. If you don't own one, you may be surprised to find out how inexpensive they are to rent. Watching your own sexy, self-loving video at a later time can be not only immensely informative but also a titillating turn-on—for you and maybe for a fortunate partner!

Woman has sex organs

just about everywhere.

She experiences pleasure

almost everywhere.

—*Luce Irigaray, This*

Sex Which Is Not One

6
g(oddess)-
spots and
love
nectars

Is there really such a thing as a G-spot? Does every woman have one? Will I be able to pinpoint mine? Can it give me a different type of orgasm? Yes, yes, yes, and *yes!* In fact, the G-spot is one of your Inner Sex Goddess's favorite treasures. She knows where yours is, and she's been eagerly waiting to initiate you and your lover into the hidden ecstasies of its potent orgasms and love nectars.

Although the ancient Romans, Japanese, Chinese, Tantric Indians, and indigenous cultures throughout history were intimately familiar with this special sweet spot inside a woman, modern society seemed to lose touch with its existence until 1950, when a German gynecologist named Ernst Grafenberg researched and wrote about it. His findings caused quite a stir among the medical and scientific crowd, but not too many other people knew about them. Then thirty years later a trio of psychologists and sex therapists expanded Grafenberg's work into a book and decided to name this ancient and utterly female body part after him—the *man* who supposedly discovered it! So it became known as the G-spot, although it does go by other, more accurate and interesting names. One woman I know affectionately calls it her love button. The Federation of Feminist Women's Health Centers refers to it, very clinically, as the urethral sponge. In Panama they speak of this savory spot as *la bella loca,* which literally means "the beautiful crazy." I like to think of it as a woman's goddess spot. Whatever it's called, this lovely hidden site is a pleasuring bonanza.

In fact, many sex researchers believe that learning to have a G-spot climax is an important key to achieving multiple orgasms. That's because after you've had one vaginal or clitoral orgasm, the extreme sensitivity of those areas will make you want to stimulate other less overwrought areas of your genital pleasure zone. Meanwhile, some doctors and psychologists are still haggling over whether women have vaginal orgasms, clitoral orgasms, or some combination of the two, or whether there even *is* a vaginal orgasm. We should do them a favor and clue them in to the fact that women have *all kinds* of orgasms, including clitoral, vaginal, G-spot, and breast! The beauty of the female body is that it's sensitive to orgasmic stimulation all over — and, yes, the G-spot is *especially* sensitive to the erotic touch, and can give you an entirely different type of orgasm than you've ever had before. It may be more subtle and somehow deeper than the ones you're used to, but maybe not; maybe your G-spot orgasms will be more electrifying or tinglier or more wavelike. Your own goddess spot mystery waits there for you to discover.

what and where is the g-spot?

Everyone has a pet theory. According to Grafenberg, the G-spot is an area in the vagina composed of the paraurethral glands and ducts, a complex network of blood vessels, nerve endings, and the tissue surrounding the neck of the bladder. The apparent function of this network is to act as a buffer between your lover's penis and your urethra by swelling and filling with blood during sexual excitement. But many doctors say the G-spot is merely a small cluster of nerve endings and blood vessels, like a little bean deep inside the vagina. And some feminist sex researchers claim it covers a lot more territory — that, in fact, it encompasses the entire complex of tissues around the urethral opening, all the way up the long bladder tube, and all around the vaginal canal.

The somewhat esoteric quality and imprecise location of any given G-spot may account for the fact that some women and their mates believe they don't have one; having been told it has to be located in one specific area, they conclude that a lack of special sensitivity there means the G-spot doesn't exist for them. How unfortunate, especially since, as we've seen, doctors and sex researchers can't even agree on where this one specific spot is! Some say it's about two inches inside the vagina, others say it's above and in back of the pubic bone, and still others say it's much deeper than that, almost at the end of the vaginal canal.

My Inner Sex Goddess and I have our own personal theory. Apparently there are very tender nerve endings associated with the urethra, at the opening and all along the bladder neck, probably designed to protect the very important function of waste removal. Since the bladder neck runs parallel to the vaginal canal, on the side toward your stomach, you can feel this tender bladder tissue through your vaginal walls. These urethral nerve endings are supersensitive in various spots along the way; and the exact location of these spots is *different for every woman.* In other words, every woman has her own personal G-spot— or even two or three G-spots!—that will look, feel, and locate itself in a manner completely unique to her. Just like everything else about a woman's sexuality, your G-spot is a highly individualized treat.

But most doctors and sexologists do seem to agree that the main function of the G-spot is to help you achieve a high degree of sexual intoxication! When you are drunk with rapture, just imagine what an uninhibited and wanton hussy you become, how much more intensely you feel even the barest touch, how much easier and more delicious it is to abandon everything to your feeling of pleasure and that of your lover. This is the special bounty of your G-spot.

How, then, do you find your special sweet spot or spots? Call on your Inner Sex Goddess to help you; she will raise your level of attunement to the subtler sensations of this area. The other helpful trick is to keep in mind the G-spot's second main function — to swell during sexual excitement for protection of the urethra and bladder. When you are aroused, the G-spot will rapidly become engorged, get harder, and may even develop well-defined edges, making it much easier to locate.

You can take the following steps to find your goddess spot:

$Step$ 1. Get yourself into a state of arousal.

$Step$ 2. Assume a seated or squatting position, like sitting on the toilet, for instance. It's almost impossible to find your sweet spots while lying on your back because gravity tends to pull your internal organs down and away from the vaginal entrance. (Remember this when you are trying to feel your G-spot during intercourse!)

$Step$ 3. Lubricate your finger and first massage gently around the urethral opening, sometimes called the meatus, not around the vaginal opening. See if and how sensitive this external area is for you. A whole new experience opened up for me when I discovered this as one of my personal goddess spots, and I couldn't understand why I'd never thought of it before. But it may not be yours, so explore carefully and with an open mind.

Step 4. Still making sure your finger is lubricated, insert it gently into your vagina. Letting yourself be guided by your instincts, use firm upward pressure to slowly investigate along the front of your internal vaginal wall. (Some women find that pressing down at the same time on the outside of the abdomen with the other hand helps pinpoint areas of special sensitivity.) Because the bladder tube runs on the other side of the front vaginal wall, you'll find your own G-spot somewhere along this path. One woman I know said she found her special spot when she felt that she was touching "an inverted clitoris, one that was inside my vagina, and much more pleasurable for me than my clitoris." But anywhere you feel a slight jolt, a momentary urge to urinate, a small, rather hard lump, or a warm, deep sensual feeling is *it*. If you don't find a G-spot right away, or even after you do, don't stop searching. You may have more than one!

Step 5. A commonly found G-spot lies about half an inch inside the vagina at about eight o'clock or four o'clock (if the top of your vagina is twelve o'clock). One woman I know found her special spot "in front and a little to right of center. When I touch it, or when my lover's penis does, it feels pleasurable and kind of liquidy."

Step 6. Be sure to try the area just above your pubic bone. As you probe inside the vagina, you first encounter the lumpy Skene's gland just inside the opening. Then there's the hard area of the pubic bone itself. Beyond it lies a smoother area leading back to the cervix. From there, come back toward the pubic bone a little and hook your finger in back of it where there's a small hollow. Wag your finger right and left. Many women find their G-spot in this area; and it is the place to which most scientists refer. But if, like me, you aren't especially sensitive right there, don't stop searching yet!

Step 7. Keep tracing your finger along the front vaginal wall, as far as you can reach. Stroke and circle with your finger. Deep inside the vagina, almost to the end, is another very common sweet spot. I especially notice mine here when my lover's penis is thrusting deep into me from behind, but it's difficult to reach with my own finger. So don't give up too soon in trying to find a possible deep sweet spot. You may want to insert a wet finger or dildo and duplicate the angle of rear-entry intercourse to fully explore the path of your goddess spot.

Step 8. Notice and remember where your sensitive spots are and how they felt when stimulated. As I've mentioned, you may have one or more G-spots; some of them may be larger than others; you may be hotly sensitive to G-spot stimulation or just mildly warmed by it; upon contact with your G-spot you may or may not have an immediate orgasm, and it may feel sharper or softer than those that are clitorally stimulated. One friend of mine describes her G-spot climaxes as "sudden, sharp, and explosive," while another says, "It feels like a warm, deep wave spreading throughout my whole body." I don't always have an orgasm when I rub my deeper G-spot, but when I do have one, it's like a slow, pulsing release. On the other hand, massaging the sweet spot at my outer urethral opening can make me feel as if I've been shot out of a cannon. Your experience will be different still.

Here's what Diane, my buttoned-down attorney friend, says about her G-spot explorations: "At first I had trouble finding my G-spot because I had this set idea about where it was supposed to be. And it just wasn't there. Then one time when Tom was making love to me from behind and we were lying on our sides, he angled into some corner of me that felt really good. The next day I pressed around inside by myself and found it again—a sort of mushy, earthy place that made me feel as if I were melting down. When I told Tom about it, he probed around with his penis until I started shuddering. This made him really hot, and he just kept thrusting into that place. Somehow this spot seemed connected to a wild animal inside me, and once it got loose, I started bucking and screaming for Tom to 'fuck

me hard!' That night we made love for hours with a feroc-
ity and urgency I'd forgotten existed in our relationship."

love nectar

When you massage your goddess spot, you may find yourself ejaculating a small amount of clear fluid from your urethra. Despite appearances, this is not urine. It is not the
color of urine, it does not smell or taste like urine, nor does it
stain like urine. Furthermore, it has now been scientifically
tested to prove it is not urine. This sweet juice is your love nectar, and it falls under the special province of Xochiquetzal,
Mayan goddess of beauty, sexuality, and flowers. Sometimes represented as a butterfly, Xochiquetzal symbolizes
the sacrament of sipping transformational ambrosia — as the
butterfly sucks the nectar of the flower, so the lover drinks
the honeyed liquid of his woman's vulva. Never be embarrassed by it; it is a lovely female ejaculation that announces
the presence of your very enjoyable orgasms.

Grafenberg observed that with women, as well as
with men, the ejaculation that occurs at orgasm involves
fluid being ejected in gushes through the urethra and that
this happens most often when the G-spot is being stimulated. Since we know that sweet spots are really urethral

nerve endings and tissues this really makes sense. It also makes sense that G-spot ejaculation is intimately related to the strength of the PC muscle, the one that controls the flow of urine. The stronger your PC muscle is, the more likely you are to emit love nectar. Some women claim they ejaculate every time they make love; others say it happens only occasionally. Some detect a cyclical pattern, possibly related to the phases of the moon. And many women never ejaculate at all and have just as good a time. So whatever your orgasmic flow experience, don't think it strange.

In fact, the female production of love nectar has been recognized and even reverently cultivated for centuries. Aristotle observed that women expelled fluid during orgasm. So did the famous second-century Greek physician Galen. And in the seventeenth century, Dutch anatomist Regnier de Graaf described the "female prostate" and "female semen" in detail. The Bataro tribe of Uganda was known to have a custom called *kachapati*, or "spray the wall," in which older women taught younger ones how to ejaculate. And in some ancient and modern Tantric teachings, sexual intercourse is said to have the specific esoteric function of stimulating the flow of female fluid, which they call *rajas*. The men of this Tantric school even make a ritual out of collecting the precious juice on a leaf, adding it to a bowl of water, offering it to the deity presiding over the ritual, and then drinking it themselves.

The taste of this orgasmic fluid has been variously described as very sweet, tangy, bitter, or tart. Not only is every woman's flavor different from that of others, but the taste of any given woman's *rajas* may change depending on her mood and the time of month. I was once lucky enough to have a lover who delighted in what he called the "sweet 'n' spicy" flavor of orgasmic juice. He loved to stimulate me to produce this nectar so that he could drink it directly from my body.

So never try to inhibit the natural flow of your precious love fluids. Remember, the Tantrics worshiped them. Try seeing yourself as they did—as the embodiment of the divine female principle, fountain of life and pleasure, source of the magical elixirs of physical and spiritual transformation—at the very least, a Sex Goddess who's so hot she overflows with the sweet nectar of love.

the goddess spot pleasure dance

Now that you've located your particular sweet spot and learned that it's perfectly okay to secrete special love juices, let's explore the best ways to incorporate the G-spot into your self-pleasuring adventures. You may find a direct shortcut to the temple of your Inner Sex Goddess.

113. It's usually best to save the G-spot for later in your pleasuring session, maybe even after you've had your initial orgasm, so that it's swollen, sensitized, and easier to find and excite. Massage, stroke, tickle, and fondle your sweet spot as you would your vaginal lips or clitoris. You will probably want to use heavier pressure on your goddess spot than you would on your clitoris, and you will probably feel the sensation deeper inside your body. Abandon yourself to its earthier tones of pleasure. You can perform this erotic dance all by itself, or you can add clitoral, nipple, or navel and tummy massage to your private party. Or simply stroke yourself all over and dream about Antonio Banderas. With the G-spot, prolonged stimulation is usually the best way to rouse your Inner Sex Goddess from her sensual slumbers.

114. The *Kama Sutra* suggests rubbing your G-spot with the middle or third finger. The ancient erotic text considers the index finger too heavy and aggressive for this delicate pleasure. Of course the middle finger is often the longest one, too—making it easier to reach your G-spot. You may also want to experiment gently with dildos, vibrators, and peeled carrots to provide a longer reach.

115. Positioning is important. Remembering that lying on your back is not the best way to find your sweet spot, you will probably correctly surmise that it's also not the best way to stimulate it. Try kneeling, squatting, or sitting on your heels with your knees apart. The positions you get into for rear-entry sex are good, too. Sandy, a friend who has created the most sumptuous bathroom I've ever seen, likes to sit on the edge of her bathtub, knees spread wide, and feet in the tub. She says this position provides a great angle for finding and rubbing the somewhat elusive love button, and she can keep her fingers wet at the tap.

116. Get on your hands and knees and use your fingers to imitate a thrusting penis bumping up against your G-spot from behind. Make sure your fingers are well lubricated and the nails trimmed. You can achieve the best angle by sliding your fingers around behind your leg and fanny, instead of approaching from the front. The rear entry and the downward motion, along with maybe a lusty "being taken" fantasy, add up to an unusually exhilarating experience.

117. If you want to learn to make love nectar, or to do so more at will, here's how. First increase your PC muscle strength and control by conscientiously doing about one hundred quick squeezes a day for at least a month. Then, in one of your self-loving sessions, get really hot and ready by giving yourself several regular orgasms with your favorite method of clitoral and vaginal stimulation. You should feel as if you're on an orgasmic plateau. Now stimulate your goddess spot with your fingers or a vibrator; if you have a sweet spot on the outside at your urethral opening, this is usually the best one to start with. Here's the key: push out and down with your vaginal muscles, rather like the way you would push with a bowel movement or when giving birth. Keep pushing as you rub, and do whatever it is that makes you so excited you feel like shaking or exploding.

David, a middle-aged accountant friend of mine, told me about the first time his wife favored him with her love juice: "First I got her incredibly hot by licking her lovely pussy until she came three times. Then I slid my two fingers just inside her opening and circled around the rough area there. She began to moan and cry 'Don't stop!' which really turned me on too. Pretty soon her vagina was pumping my fingers, almost shoving them out. And then she squirted the most delicious warm liquid all over my hand. I loved it!" The important things to take note of here are her high level of arousal, the sweet-spot massage, and the shoving that she did. These are the keys to making a successful and exciting brew of goddess love nectar, either by yourself or with your man. Happy trails!

7

fantasies from the cloud damsels

$f$antasizing is as natural as walking, sleeping, and breathing. In fact, we can't seem to stop doing it. And why would we want to? The exciting sensory images that come unbidden from our subconscious, from the heart of our most intimate erotic reservoirs, are as necessary to our lives as the bread we eat, yet as naughtily delicious as chocolate candy. They make our skin tingle, our hearts flutter, and our deep inner caves moisten. And like magic carpets, they transport us to enchanted realms of raging desire, perfect love, and unashamed carnality.

The goings-on in our heads—our attitudes, beliefs, personal rules and regulations, wishes and dreams—are at the very source of who we really are. They keep us posted on who we think we are now, who we'd like to be, who we'd like to "try on" for five minutes, and who we'd like our partners to be. And they determine who we *will* be, if we so desire. Erotic, irrational, and completely carefree, this private world is ours alone—unassailable by anyone else's opinions or needs, undemanding of anyone else's presence or good graces, unfathomable to anyone else's linear everyday thinking. Our personally fabricated mythology constitutes an intimate inner fortress and playground that gives us strength, joy, and freedom. For even if we can't quite manage to let ourselves go stark raving wild in our jobs, relationships, and bedchambers, our fantasies give us the opportunity to visit a land where letting it all hang out is deliciously de rigueur.

These exotic passports to otherwise forbidden erotic territory are issued by the ethereal Cloud Damsels who float through our imagination. Erotic nature spirits who live in a lofty dimension parallel to human reality, the Cloud Damsels, known as Apsaras in Hindu and Buddhist mythology, are sacred beings of both earth and sky. Originally human women but now goddesses (like you!), their special gift is the ability to combine sensuous flesh with divinity, sexuality with spirituality, fantasy with reality. With their fluid, sweet-smelling bodies, they may take one human lover or hundreds of godlike consorts, effortlessly combining the earthy sensuality of one with the impossibly wild and divine imaginings of the other, and vice versa. Tall, ornate headdresses sprout from their temples like the abundant fruitfulness of their erotic imagination. They delight in spicing up any and all sexual encounters with a tidbit of juicy fantasy, elevating the mundane to the glorious, human sweat to divine ambrosia, and solo sex to a magnificent garden richly populated with amorous Greek Adonises, dashing and swarthy sheikhs, and insatiable young sexpots of the male, female, animal, and extraterrestrial persuasion.

The Cloud Damsels, as close companions to your

Inner Sex Goddess, live in the most uninhibited and un-censored part of your mind. There they are free to reflect the vivid images of your raciest thoughts, your most inti-mate desires, and your most deeply hidden pleasure stimulators without having to bother with the complica-tions of real life, real people, or real consequences. They give you the freedom to indulge in any outrageous scenario you care to—being penetrated by a huge black stallion, making oral love to another woman, having wild sex with Björn Borg on Wimbledon's center court as thousands of horny onlookers applaud—while still keeping your mar-riage, your self-esteem, your emotions, and your pocket-book intact. What a divine luxury!

While the five physical senses are potent conveyances to the realm of your Inner Sex Goddess, fantasizing can be thought of as the sixth, vitalizing sense. Under the purview of the otherworldly Cloud Damsels, it's the sense that en-hances all the others, opening up even more diverse ave-nues for your unfettered sexuality, and, as Nancy Friday says in *My Secret Garden*, "taking one further, faster in the direction in which the unashamed unconscious already knows it wants to go." Your creative and erotic imagina-tion is the sense that can intuit, interpret, and invent intan-gibles—like romance, atmosphere, mystery, intoxicating danger, forbidden delights, and irrational, all-consuming lust—all the things that stimulate our particularly female hormones. For we women are creatures of rhapsody and enigma, more stimulated by emotion than by action, more aroused by the romance of sex than by the mechanics of sex, and more unloosed by imagination than by facts, formulas, and graphic realities. We come fully alive in our fantastical imaginings.

That's why your Inner Sex Goddess recommends investing *every* sensual activity with erotic imagery—exploratory sessions with your body, sybaritic warm-ups for sex, partner lovemaking, and especially self-pleasuring, where it's just you and your unbridled imagination. As the Cloud Damsels in you know, all of these fleshly pleasures can be even further glorified by healthy dollops of divinely inspired phantasm. And in this rarefied atmosphere of magical reality, *anything* goes. There is nothing to be ashamed of, for your daydreams, reveries, and mental inventions simply reflect your unique, and completely normal, sexual personality—uncensored, rare, courageous, and exquisitely precious. You don't have to act them out, tell them to anyone, or even figure them out. On the other hand, you can do all of those things if it would please and excite you to do so. Your flights of fancy are your private possessions to invent, modify, reveal, conceal, discard, repeat, and indulge in as you will.

having a pleasant flight

When you allow yourself to travel to the vast open spaces of fantasyland, you will find your sensual life taking on a new radiance. Women who give free rein to their Cloud Damsel visions report that their experience of sex is more intense, more ecstatic, and more full-bodied than they ever thought possible. In fact, many women say they can achieve orgasm by fantasy alone, with no physical stimulation at all. The key is to surrender completely to the irrational brilliance of your own erotic mind and to let your fantasies lead you, not the other way around. Here are some tips for making the most of your fantasy flights:

- Impose no limits. While few of us would actually have sex in the middle of Times Square, fantasizing about it can be delicious, healthy fun. So don't label yourself a pervert or nymphomaniac just because you like to dream about being trussed up, blindfolded, and ravaged by twenty-seven Mongol warriors. On the contrary, be as outrageous and outlandish as you possibly can. Enjoy the rare opportunity to explore the impossible and to step into someone else's skin — whether it be Venus de Milo, Irma la Douce, a nymphomaniac mermaid, a tightly laced Victorian damsel aching to have her bodice ripped, a primitive cave-woman, a creature from *Star Wars*, or even a male truck driver with "horns." Whatever your weirdest fantasy, there are at least a thousand completely normal women out there whose kinky castle-building is even more over-the-top than yours. So let your unfettered hallucinations bring out all of your muskiest natural perfumes, your most salacious proclivities, and your wildest primal instincts. Make no judgments. Take no prisoners or guilt trips. These private tours are safe within the boundaries of your head and heart.

• I think it's best *not* to share your fantasies with your mate. He might feel threatened, intimidated, outraged, or even betrayed, especially if his delicate male ego is called into question. Worse yet, he might criticize or belittle your fanciful efforts, puncturing a gigantic hole in your fantasy balloon. But most important, if you know someone else will be privy to your secret exotic dreams, you will not feel free to indulge in the really juicy, borderline ones—the most liberating and fun visions of all!

The exceptions to this are those fantasies that you specifically want to turn into reality and that you feel are safe, nonthreatening, and practical enough to do so. I once conjured up a vision of taking my lover to the opera, both of us dressed to the nines, and slipping off for a stand-up quickie in some dark corner while the onstage drama raged on. The elegance, furtiveness, and danger of this make-believe scenario really appealed to my naughty Inner Sex Goddess—and to my man, when I shared it with him. For months it was a joint fantasy that we used to titillate each other. Then one night at the theater, he got up in the middle of the first act and led me to a vestibule, where, behind a swinging door, we pounded into each other until we heard the audience applaud and begin to leave the theater proper. Just in the nick of time, we refastened our clothes and nonchalantly emerged from behind the door to join the exiting audience for intermission. It was fantastic, but then I had to think up a new outrageous daydream!

• Fantasize at every opportunity—while commuting on the train, lying in the sun, ironing tablecloths, enduring a meeting, fixing dinner, observing a flower, drifting off to sleep, showering, flying on a plane, walking to work, and especially when looking at and touching your body or that of your lover. Fantasize while you are preparing for a sensual encounter, making love to your man, or indulging in your favorite self-pleasuring activities. The more you flex your fantasy muscles, the more alive you will feel, the more abandoned and creative a lover you will be, and the better you will know your Inner Sex Goddess, for it is in the realm of your vivid imagination that she lives, breathes, and grows.

• Use props. Make your fantasies as real as possible by adding a dash of tactile reality—a filmy scarf for your harem sojourn (while in Egypt I bought scads of sheer belly-dancing scarves with dangling beadwork just for that purpose); a furry tail for your Catwoman reverie; a length of rope or a blindfold for your "rape" fantasies; mesh stockings and a brief, frilly apron for the French maid in you; sandalwood or musk incense for imaginary Tantric rituals; juicy fruits for fantasy love with Tom Jones. And of course always have your favorite toys readily available—vibrators, videos, scented massage oil, ben wa balls, and so forth. Your castles in the air become much more erotically solid when draped with the stuff of reality.

• Let your erotic visions speak a different language. In fantasies, men don't have "penises"; they flaunt swollen "cocks." You no longer own a "bosom" and "genitals"; now you've got creamy "tits" and a "juicy pussy." And horny hunks don't swarm around to have "intercourse" with you; they are panting to "fuck" you silly. For many of us, the brazen language of sex can instantly trigger your most wanton instincts and transform your fantasies from bland into sizzling. Foreign words, too, can add just the right touch of exotic romance when you are daydreaming about sexy Italian counts or rough-hewn blond Vikings. Phrases such as *"Baise-moi, chéri!" "Bums Mich Schneller, Liebling!"* and *"Chiavami, tesoro!"* are just the ticket to exciting foreign fantasylands. Learn to savor these powerfully evocative words. Whisper them to yourself in the dark of night. Chant them to yourself. Use them to catapult otherwise casual musings into the realm of hot, depraved fantasy masterpieces.

going to the source

I am in the African bush with an untamed lover. We roll in the leaves and wallow in the mud like languorous primitive beasts, and then he washes me off in a cool green river. We glide through the water on the back of an alligator, and when the creature tries to reach around and devour me, my wild lover saves me from its cruel jaws with the power of his muscled arms. He proudly parades me through the village, naked on the back of a giant wrinkled elephant. In his hut he leaves me bare but wraps himself up in white robes so that I can see only his dark smoldering eyes as they travel hotly over my quivering nakedness. Then he parts his robes for me so I can touch his hot, hard body, and I kneel down to take his swollen member in my mouth. Caressing my head as I suck him, he brings me under his robes, where it's even hotter than under the African sun. He pours his honeyed come down the front of my body and rubs it into my breasts so that I'll bear his scent. Slowly we sink down onto the rough mat, and he enters me from behind, biting my neck and growling softly like a wild animal. His huge shaft plunges hard against the very deepest part of my woman's well, and soon I am panting in uncontrolled ecstasy. Hours pass as he keeps me teetering on the brink of breathless release. Finally, possessing me completely by reaching around to put one hand on my throbbing bud and the other on a burning hot nipple, he thrusts even more powerfully into me, snarling like a great tiger—and I scream in the ecstatic agony of my body's surrender. Later he bathes me under a cascading waterfall and lies with me on the banks of the river, while we listen to the hyenas laugh.

■

One night, while out dancing in a tight red dress, I am suddenly grabbed by three men who blindfold me and throw me into the back of a van. Days later, awaking from the drugs they've given me, I find myself standing on the auction block of a white slave market. I am covered from head to toe with robes; only my eyes are visible. The auctioneer says, "The bidding will start at one million rupees for this exceptionally fine specimen!" Suddenly he rips away my robes, exposing my entire naked body; the audience gasps in excited approval. Several customers, men dressed in long robes and turbans, come up and bounce my breasts between their hands, pinch my nipples, and grab my bottom. One man in a blue sash even rubs my clit and thrusts an incredibly long finger deep inside me, pumping it in and out to observe my reaction. Though I should feel humiliated and angry, I find myself feeling haughty and sexy instead, because I can see that every one of these men has a huge erection jutting out under his robe. I start gyrating my hips, squeezing my own tits, and massaging my pussy. I look right into the eyes of the man with the blue sash and lick my lips suggestively. I take my fingers out of my wet sex and stick them in his mouth. He starts sucking them hungrily and whips out his iron rod to get at it with his hands. All the other men do the same, so that all I see are these gorgeous shafts aching and throbbing for me. I am turned on tremendously, and I keep undulating and fucking myself with my fingers until all of those men spurt their come all over my body—all except the man in the blue sash: he sticks his stone-hard member straight up my pussy and fucks me hard, fast, and deep, right there in front of everybody, and I explode in uncontrollable spasms. I select him as my lucky owner and lead him off to demand more fucking.

Though some women quite easily and prolifically conjure up elaborate visions like the ones above to accompany their self-pleasuring interludes, many of us are just as happy dreaming up much simpler scenarios—like "What would my next-door neighbor look like without his clothes? I'll bet his stomach muscles ripple, all the way down to his . . ." or "I'd love to rub my oiled-up breasts all over my husband's body." That's okay. Fantasies can run the gamut from simple musings about real men and situations to complicated visions of exotic lands, strangely sexed people, and bizarre or impossible copulations. Almost anything you see, read, hear about, remember, or experience can become a rich source of voluptuous inner visions for you. The world, and especially the sensualized domain that your Inner Sex Goddess perceives, is full of juicy ideas. So never feel stumped as to where and how to come up with really tasty fantasy material. Simply tune your otherwise rational brain in to the outlandishly opulent wavelength of your personal Cloud Damsels and view the world through their erotic-tinted glasses. Allow yourself to recognize a sensual image when you see one, relish it, take a mental picture of it, write about it in your journal, free-associate it with any people, places, or things that float across your mind. Let your imagination range freely over completely new territory. Then, when next you want to embody your Inner Sex Goddess—whether you are self-pleasuring, making love to your man, or standing in line at the bank—flip through your mental catalog of self-produced fantasy flicks and plug in the hottest one.

118. Recall a man, situation, or previous lovemaking session that made your love button shiver. In your mind, savor the sounds, smells, and textures that went with it. Embellish them. In your imagination let them evolve to an extreme pleasure point. Here's an example: "I had a lover once who had the most beautiful smooth brown skin. Just the smell of it drove me insane with lust. Whenever I want to get hot, I remember that musky scent and the feel of his skin against my chest. Sometimes I get to swimming in that smell and imagine that it's pouring in through my nose, mouth, and vagina to fill every corner of my body. It turns my insides to warm honey." And another: "My boyfriend and I used to jump on his motorcycle and go for wild moonlight rides. Remembering the feel of that vibrating hunk of metal and my boyfriend's ass between my legs makes me tremble even now. It works especially well in tandem with my vibrator."

119. Read steamy novels. Become one of the characters and immerse yourself in the hottest scenes—clothes, food, toys, locales, the whole megillah. Some of those anonymous Victorian porn books can be delightfully kinky—with wide-eyed, pantalooned maidens turning into sex-crazed, riding crop–wielding mistresses who love to watch their brothers impale every servant in the house. Or become a different sex. "Henry Miller's books really get my juices flowing," a friend told me. "I love to put on my husband's clothes—when he's not around, of course—and pretend I'm one of Miller's cocky male heroes, throwing around words like 'prick' and 'pussy' and whipping out my huge member to fuck every woman who crosses my path. It's fun to wear the shoe on the other foot for a change."

120. Peruse adult magazines. The photos, especially in *Penthouse,* are often meant to be realistic fantasies. A ten-page layout of two women playing with ice dildos supplied me with raw fantasy material for months. Don't forget to read the stories and the letters from other readers too. "A man wrote in about secretly watching his wife shed all her inhibitions and have pornographic sex with two hunky gardeners, and for some reason that lit all my fuses," my friend Mary told me. "Improvising my own version, I have great fun imagining my husband spying on me as I have my way with the virile young guys who clean our pool. My favorite part is when I sit on the lap of one, his love-stick buried deep inside me and my back to him, while the other guy slurps on my clit. This is just too much for my husband, and he has to come out of hiding and join in by sucking my tits. Of course I would never do this in real life, but that's what makes it even more fun to fantasize about!"

121. Walk in nature. When you see a waterfall, fancy that you are standing under it with a long-haired Polynesian lover, feeling the water and his hands on your breasts. Let the intense mossy green of a forest return home with you as a mental talisman that evokes vivid color, moist earthy feelings, and romantic medieval imagery. See mountains as breasts to suckle, trees and skyscrapers as mighty shafts to penetrate you, rock clefts as mouths to kiss and be kissed by. Let a mud puddle conjure up visions of rolling in the mud with a crocodile, a wolf, or a primitive tribal lover. Use these natural spices to flavor your solo or partner lovemaking. One nature lover I know told me this fantasy. "All of a sudden this log became a platform on which I could display myself to hundreds of men. In my mind, I lay back on it, nude, the log between my legs so that I was spread-eagled, my sex open wide. I could imagine the bark prickling my bare back and ass as I massaged my juicy opening, and all these men with huge naked erections stared at me hungrily. But no one was allowed to touch me because I was the sacred white goddess of the forest, and they had to worship me from afar."

122. Become another woman—someone you've read about, seen in a movie, or heard of in a song. "I have different fantasy personalities depending on the activity," a woman told me. "For pleasuring myself, I mentally play the role of Salome, whom I see as someone unashamed of touching her body and with lots of marvelous veils and things to play with. With my husband, I imagine that I am Xaviera Hollander, the Happy Hooker, flaunting my bold sexuality and giving him everything a man could possibly dream of. And when I just want to relieve the boredom of ironing, I invent a scene where I'm 'Brown Sugar' from that Rolling Stones song. She's a saucy little tart who drives all kinds of rock stars wild."

123. When you see an attractive man, imagine what he looks and feels like naked. What outrageous things would he do to you? What naughty acts would you perform for him? How would his penis be shaped? What color is his pubic hair? Does he have a tattoo on his right inner thigh? Would he like to shave your mound? How does the inside of his mouth taste? Would he prefer you in white cotton, red lace, or black leather? Does he cry out when he comes? Are his nipples sensitive? his earlobes? his eyelids? Would he have a penchant for licking your cleavage? Would you like to lick his? The next time you play with your vibrator, imagine it's his hands that are giving you those sudden shocks of pleasure.

124. Read sex manuals. Pick out some of the kinkier suggestions that you might never have the nerve to do in real life—like having your man whip you lovingly, wrapping his penis with pearls, or inviting a third person

into your love-play—and fantasize about them. Devise your own variations. Pretend that you are being photographed or drawn for the book's illustrations. As you fill your mind with these vivid images, let them stir you into self-pleasuring action. "I've always read about watching yourself have sex in an overhead mirror, but I'd be too embarrassed to do this with my husband. So sometimes when we make love, or especially when I'm by myself, I imagine that I can see the reflection of his tidy little rear bouncing up and down on top of me. It gives me the most amazing tingles," a friend told me.

125. Be alert for accidental triggers to your erotic imagination. Wrong numbers, incorrectly addressed mail, switched luggage or tickets, accidental grocery cart collisions, misinterpreted words or names, and unusually striking newspaper articles can all carry the seeds of a great fantasy garden. I used to get occasional wrong-number phone calls from people asking for Natasha. Eventually, one deeply disappointed caller told me that Natasha was a dominatrix who had always had this phone number, and maybe I'd like to get paid for "punishing" him instead of just insisting that this "bad boy" had reached the wrong number! I hung up on him and got my phone number changed, but in the meantime I had great fun fantasizing about rudely making appointments with these men—how they would love the verbal abuse!—putting on hip boots and chains, and satisfying their every desire for erotic leather punishment.

126. Let music shape your feelings into images. Brazilian music or reggae can take you to hot tropical climes where small bikinis, dark sultry men, and devil-may-care attitudes have free rein. The heavy drumbeat of hard rock may stir your primitive instincts. Baroque sonatas may turn you into a bird flying free of all society's limitations or a guitar being plucked by a man's strong fingers. "I don't fantasize about people or events but more about feelings," Carol told me. "I can put on a piece of music, concentrate on a particular instrument or melody line, and use that to focus my sensations and feelings into one electric-blue chord that flows throughout my body as I want it to. This chord feels hot, cold, and throbbing all at the same time, and it kind of beams into my hands, breasts, and genitals as the music trips along. It intensifies everything that I'm doing to myself, and if I focus it in my clitoris, it always gives me an orgasm."

127. Advertisements are a great source of fantasy these days. How about those Calvin Klein ads showing the naked torso of a perfectly sculpted man on the sand? Imagine rolling in the waves with him or feeling the bulge in his jeans. The ads for Guess jeans often depict a hot western scenario or a coffee-shop tête-à-tête with gorgeous men and women lolling about. You could walk right into one of those scenes and get branded by your favorite cowboy. TV commercials for perfume are usually designed specifically to evoke romantic fantasies: Liz Taylor seductively bringing luck to some classy dude in a casino; a pouty-lipped woman challenging you that "not every woman can wear Red," apparently because it's so hot and bold; some Fabio look-alike galloping up on a horse to scoop you up and away to cloudland. And then there's the next-door neighbor who comes to borrow coffee. My friend Teresa fantasizes, "That sexy hunk rings my chimes all right. When he comes to ask for coffee, I invite him in, and while I'm reaching up to get the tin off the shelf, he comes up behind me, pins me against the cupboard, raises my skirt, and screws the living daylights out of me. Then I undo his shirt, put honey on his nipples, and lick it off, and somehow we forget all about the coffee."

 / 2 8. Delve into your dreams for fantasy scenarios. As messages from the subconscious, dreams can give us clues to the "forbidden" desires and fears we otherwise keep hidden from ourselves, and in fantasy it's safe to explore them. I once had a powerfully erotic dream about the very ordinary man who was my boss at the time. Although in real life I liked and respected him, there had been no particular sexual chemistry between us—and it would have been a career disaster to get romantically involved with him. But in my nocturnal imagining, I let myself see the suave and sexy Don Juan personality that he probably never revealed even to himself and that lit a huge bonfire in my libido. Intentionally refraining from any real-life dalliance with him, I undressed him with my eyes and made dangerously abandoned imaginary love to him in the hallway for months. It made going to work such a treat!

You can also program your dreams to work things out for you. A friend told me she'd been having mental flashes of two of her female colleagues licking and biting her all over. She did not want to explore the idea of making love to a woman in real life, but these images were so persistent that she decided to tackle the idea in her dreams. After about five nights of falling to sleep deliberately thinking about these women, she finally had a dream in which the three of them made an intensely erotic porn movie together, stroking, sucking, tweaking, and kissing each other in every possible entangled combination. She enjoyed the dream so much, and it felt so natural to her, that she treasured it as a favorite fantasy for years. Even though she still had no desire for same-sex love in her daily life, she allowed herself to relish the beauty of woman in her dreams and fantasies.

$129.$ Assign yourself a role—any role—and see where it takes you.

- You're a librarian who just can't help sneaking hunky young college students in between the shelves for some real education.
- You're a sports reporter, and when you find yourself in the football players' locker room, you tear off all your clothes and massage yourself to orgasm while the entire team cheers.
- You're a teenager on your first date, making out for hours, then finally letting him feel your breast, his hot, desperate panting loud in your ear.
- You're stranded on a desert isle with only the wild animals for loving company.
- You're a harem girl, pampered, perfumed, bathed, and licked by hundreds of beautiful lusty women every day and chosen to suck the sultan's golden dagger every night.
- You're a porn film star and have to watch hugely endowed men and beautifully molded women having sex constantly; then you let three men and two women suck, fuck, and bite you for ninety-seven camera takes.
- You're a nineteenth-century French maid whose master often finds it necessary to spank you for dereliction of duty.
- You're a Tantrica in an ancient Oriental garden pungent with the smell of orange blossoms and jasmine, and an Indian god with twelve arms smooths

every inch of your body with his twelve hands while making transcendental love to you.

• You're an executive at a meeting, and one of your colleagues has slipped under the conference table to lick you between the legs.

• You're a hostage who is tied down, forced to perform cunnilingus on six women, spanked with the thick penises of ten huge men, and then taken from behind by each one in turn.

• You're Lady Godiva, riding bareback and bare-assed through town with only your long tresses to cover your voluptuous charms.

• You have a blind date, and you're getting dressed to go meet a new man for the first time, dreaming up all his sensational qualities and odd quirks, anticipating the flirtatious eye signals and dinner conversation, imagining all the salacious things he might try to (and you might let him) do to you.

• You're a despotic ruler whose male subjects must pay tribute to you by sucking your nipples and then rubbing their come all over your body.

• You're a glamorous gambler at a casino in Monaco, and a visiting Italian prince follows you around the casino all night and finally whisks you off to his yacht for a moonlight tryst.

• You're a waitress at an elegant restaurant who occasionally slips into the men's room and has sex with whoever is in there, no matter how many or how few.

• You're a bee who has ecstatic orgasms by flying deep into the well of fragrant, brilliantly colored flowers and rolling gleefully around in their soft golden pollen.

cloud damsel visions

While most fantasies are purely for lustful fun, a certain kind of imagining is meant for more serious business—the business of designing reality the way you want it to be. Whether that means making changes in the way your partner feels and behaves, making changes in the way you feel and behave, or calling a new lover to you, these visions are fantasies with a powerful purpose. Indulge in them often enough, and you will find your real life starting to take the shape of your utopian dreams. It's as if you and your Cloud Damsels sit around a white witches' magic cauldron: you throw in mental pictures of what you want, together you brew it up with imagination, and the resulting steam carries your desires to their intended destination in reality, infusing the person or thing with the smoky essence of your erotic vision. More potent than ordinary visualizations, these magnetic mirages carry all the power of your fervid physical desire, hotly charged emotion, and most unbridled imagination. Your inner voices will prompt you when it's appropriate to use them.

130. Imagine summoning a lover to you. When my friend Vivian wants to bring a new man into her life or make a long-distance connection with a current one, she merely thinks intensely of that person while she pleasures her body. She feels herself calling to him energetically and sees the man consciously receiving the connection. Vivian says this seems to work even better for her when done in the shower because her pleasure is more intense and because she envisions the steam from her very hot, wet body floating off with the powerful erotic magic of her dream. When I tried this once, I not only had a deliciously entertaining shower, but the lover I'd been thinking of phoned me from three thousand miles away immediately after I left the bathroom!

131. Design beautiful new feelings about your own body that will translate into bewitching behavior. Because I believe it's so important for women to learn to love and admire their genitals, I often recommend they try autoerotic play enhanced with the following fantasy: Envisage your mate or imaginary lover ardently licking the lips of your sex and moaning, "I love your gorgeous pussy. It tastes sooooo good and makes me so hard." As your passion mounts, he kisses you even more intensely and groans, "Give me more of your delicious nectar. I love to lap it up." Embroider on this basic scenario as you wish and allow your hands or vibrator to act it out. In addition to being delectable self-pleasuring fun, this vision helps you (1) to know in your bones what a magical, sexy jewel your vulva is; (2) to radiate physical heat from your sex organs to those of your lover; and (3) to invent elegantly lewd pelvic moves.

132. Fantasize your mate into the Valentino-like lover you desire. Suppose your man, though he means well, just doesn't spend enough time on foreplay. You've tried retraining him with erotic massage, seductive self-pleasuring shows, and tender talk, but you've had only moderate success. Time for voluptuous visions. In a private pleasuring session, imagine that your once-reluctant lover is now slowly teasing you in all the sweetly agonizing ways you crave. In vivid detail, see him lovingly massage your toes; feel his slow, sensuous caress on your inner thigh; smell the scent of his fevered skin as he bites your nipple; hear the passionate endearments he whispers in your ear; taste his tangy tongue on the corners of your mouth. Simultaneously, inflame all these hot spots with your own loving hands, building your excitement to a feverish heat. The combination of the powerful creative juices of sex, your steaming emotions, and your fierce intention will drive this blazing message straight into your lover's heart.

And then it happened like a miracle, this pulsation of pleasure unequalled by the most exalted musicians, the summits of perfection in art or science or wars, unequalled by the most regal beauties of nature, this pleasure which transformed the body into a high tower of fireworks gradually exploding into fountains of delight through the senses.

—Anaïs Nin

8

the secrets of divine orgasm

We women know that orgasm is not a *goal* to be achieved at all costs, like a touchdown or a home run. In fact, sometimes we don't even care if we have an orgasm because we enjoy the sweet ecstasy of the *process* of lovemaking so much. Yet that pleasure "unequalled by the most regal beauties of nature" is a divine gift to which we are most definitely entitled, and which your Inner Sex Goddess most dearly wishes to bestow upon you. In fact, the blissful waves of orgasm are vital food for the goddesses within your body, strengthening all your subtle energy centers and nourishing your physical and mental capabilities as well. The ecstatic pulsations of your orgasm also constitute one of the most deeply satisfying gifts you can give your lover. Few things turn a man on more than knowing he has solved the eternal mystery, found the elusive Grail, and sent your body into uncontrolled spasms of rapture—which then cascade all over *his* body.

We Sex Goddesses have this divine frenzy well within our power—to receive and to give. The research of Masters and Johnson indicates that women's capacity for orgasm far exceeds that of men. And the more we exercise this ability, the more sensitive and responsive to orgasmic stimuli we become, achieving even greater heights of climactic ecstasy, capacity, and skill. In fact, Mary Jane Sherfey in *The Nature and Evolution of Female Sexuality* speculates that without the restraints of societal and internal taboos, women might be freed to behave more naturally, in a similar fashion to our close relatives the higher primates who copulate, and probably reach orgasm, up to fifty times a day when in heat. How happy and healthy they and their mates must be!

Not too far removed from this state of natural, sexually vibrant well-being are the islanders of Mangaia in central Polynesia. Believed to be the most orgasmically advanced society in the world, they consider female orgasm not an indulgence but a necessity. At puberty, Mangaian males are taught how to stimulate women to maximum sexual pleasure, and the man who fails to give his woman at least two orgasms every time they make love loses his status in the island's society. Sadly, our culture is not so advanced.

But actually it's much better to retain control of your own body and its pleasures anyway, to realize that nobody *gives* you orgasms. You create them yourself by knowing how your body reaches its peak and then directing your feelings and activities in a way that *allows* an orgasm to occur. This command of simultaneous control and abandon is the special talent and gift of your Inner Sex Goddess and of the many sex goddesses, ancient and modern, who have discovered the secrets of first-time, dependably regular, teeth-chattering, and multiple orgasm and have honed their skills into a fine art. Let's listen in on one of their powwows.

Once upon a time a group of ancient priestesses and modern-day sex goddesses sat around the campfire trying to figure out how to induce the Goddess Who Makes You Shudder Inside to visit them. They knew she could be elusive and that she required praise and petting that met certain very high standards. But these women had clues and secrets that they whispered to each other over the fire. "Try rubbing very fast." "Let yourself go." "Maybe worshiping a cucumber will make her come," they said. And lo, the mysterious seeds of their shared female wisdom eventually bore fruit, the Goddess Who Makes You Shudder Inside appeared full bloom in their midst, and they and their lucky mates lived ecstatically ever after. Each in her turn had revealed a secret. . . .

Secret # 1

Know and Love Your Sexual Self—Regularly.

This, of course, is what you've been doing throughout this book—exploring your body and finding not its faults but all of its sexy hollows and curves; discovering your personal hot spots, desires, and sexual style; becoming intimate with your Inner Sex Goddess; loving your sensuality, your wild erotic thoughts, and your genitals; learning how to pleasure yourself, and thereby your lover. As one woman said, "I never had an orgasm until I gathered up the courage to look at my vagina, decided it was beautiful and lovable, and finally got comfortable touching myself and feeling a little bit out of control. That's when all heaven broke loose."

A woman who loves her sexuality and regularly pleasures herself to orgasm has a high degree of sexual self-confidence. She wants to express herself sexually more than the usual woman and possesses a higher-than-average sensual thermostat. She likes her body and thinks of herself as lovable and valuable. She expects to delight herself and her lover more than the ordinary woman would; and she most often does. Her self-pleasure is its own reward. Yet it's because she's so hot that she gets the best lovers and the best loving. "When I realized that *I* am the one, not a man, who brings sexuality into my life, I felt as if I had been reborn. My body, now truly my own, seemed very precious and powerful. It showed me how to have *real* orgasms."

Secret #2

Surrender.

Wilhelm Reich, the psychoanalyst who wrote *The Function of the Orgasm,* described climax as "the ability to surrender to the flow of sexual energy without any inhibition." Abandoning yourself to your hot-blooded feelings is essential if you want to be carried over the orgasmic edge, for the very essence of orgasm is letting go, relinquishing control, being lost in the moment, submitting to your body's imperative. You must ask your critical, control-freak self to step aside and let your voluptuous feelings show the way. One very wise woman said, "You can't *force* yourself to orgasm; you have to relax, get in the flow, and let your body do its own thing." And yet another has said, "I get myself as excited as possible and then just let go. I kind of surrender to my sensations."

Secret #3

Focus.

Every orgasmic woman I know says she intoxicates herself to orgasm by throwing everything else out of her mind and concentrating only on her body and its heady feelings of pleasure. At that moment nothing else exists. "I empty my mind and merge with my feelings," one woman told me. "When I touch my breasts, I concentrate fiercely on the tips of my nipples. When I stroke my vagina, I am so focused there that I *become* my vagina, pulsing and contracting." This ability to loose yourself from the bonds of normal reality and focus totally on the altered reality of voluptuous sensation is what allows many women to achieve extraordinary or multiple orgasmic peaks. "In my private world, only the tip of my clitoris exists. But at that moment it feels bigger than my whole body, as if I'm one giant clitoris rippling on waves of vibration."

Secret #4

Get the Right Kind of Clitoral Stimulation — and Plenty of It.

Whether you like it direct or indirect, fast or slow, hard or easy, with water or your hand or a vibrator, find out what drives your clitoris crazy—and stick with it until your body can't stand the agonizing pleasure anymore and has to climax to relieve the tension. One friend says, "My best orgasms happen when I spread my vaginal lips apart and let the faucet in the tub run full blast right on my clit. The faucet is fabulous and can last a lot longer than I can." Another self-educated woman chimes in, "I like to move a vibrator up and down over my clitoris for about ten minutes nonstop. Then I just hold it steady and push it in until I explode." Still another says, "I can accelerate my orgasm by holding the sides of my clitoral hood between my finger and thumb and gently massaging it while I slide a wet finger over the tip of the clitoris itself. Fireworks!"

Secret #5

Try Your Goddess Spot.

Wherever it is, your G-spot is *your* area of special sensitivity, so capitalize on it. Three different sex goddesses say: "I arch my back so my fingers can reach a real deep sexy place inside me. Then just a couple of strokes and I go off like a cannon." "I can come several times if I put a dildo just inside my vagina and rub it up and down quickly over that rough spot I love." "My G-spot is outside over my urethra. If I massage it in circles, orgasmic waves start right away."

Secret #6

Flex Your PC Muscle.

Contracting the PC muscle greatly increases sensation and adds enough additional stimulation to bring many women to the threshold of orgasm. One wild maiden confides, "Tightening makes the feelings stronger. When I get close to climaxing, I squeeze hard and hold my vaginal walls together till the contractions stop." And another says, "After I have an orgasm, I use my PC to mimic the contractions until I come again."

Secret #7

Watch Yourself in the Mirror.

Many women are tantalized into orgasm by seeing what their own buildup of sexual tension looks like and watching how their body moves with mild or intense orgasms. One says, "When I see my vaginal lips swelling, opening up like a hothouse flower and undulating real sexy-like, I start quivering inside and sort of roll into an internal shudder." Another autoerotic voyeur declares, "My nipples get very dark and big, as if someone's been kissing and biting them for hours. And then my whole body seems to get pink and light up. Watching this sends me right over the edge."

Secret #8

Use a Vibrator.

This secret is especially helpful if you've never had an orgasm. But even if you have, new sensual peaks await you, as the following story illustrates. "A friend told me about the fun she was having with her vibrator, and I wanted to explore too. It was great because I could direct the intense pulsing movements exactly where I wanted them and keep them going for a really long time. I felt that I was building up to some sort of explosion or precipice, and I remember thinking, Could this be dangerous? Soon I felt as if I'd reached the top of some mountain and then fallen off into a blissful state of delicious inner pulsing and uncontrollable contractions that I had never dreamed my body was capable of." (See Chapter 9 for details on using vibrators.)

Secret #9

Fantasize.

The most erotic organ in the body is your brain. It is the epicenter of your sexual earthquakes. And as you know from the previous chapter, your personal Cloud Damsels are intimately familiar with the wilds of your interior erotic terrain. In the blink of an eye, they can create at least ten hot fantasies that will expertly touch off any number of private landslides. So do as more than 80 percent of orgasmic women do: fire up your imagination to bring on a shuddering orgasm. Here's what just one of them said, "I like to get on all fours with a vibrator beneath me on a pillow and imagine that I am being taken doggie-style. This wonderful little fantasy brings on multiple orgasms and makes me really hot for more loving from my real-life man." Another creative vamp shares this fantasy: "I lie flat on my back, insert three wet fingers, and fantasize that an Arab prince has whisked me off to his tent and laid me down on a long table covered with luscious exotic foods. The women of his harem start licking me all over like a piece of fruit, and the prince himself slips his tongue deep inside me. That always makes me come right away!"

Secret # 10

Play a Role.

Sometimes playing the part of a sex kitten, a dominatrix, or an innocent young girl can free the wildly orgasmic you from the bonds that restrain her. Dress the part and really act it out. Three playful Sarah Bernhardts confide: "When I wear my red lace bra and see-through panties, I start slinging my hips around and getting naughty. I feel like a high-class call girl capable of firing off a hundred orgasms." "I like to dress up like Lolita, with red pouty lips and little schoolgirl dresses. Then I do that 'shy Di' look. Sexy and sweet at the same time, I feel it's okay to do anything, including innocently losing control of my body and, 'Oh my! I've just had an orgasm!' " "I *pretend* that I'm having an incredibly intense orgasm. I shout and fling myself around in a frenzy. My body doesn't seem to know the difference and actually comes to a climax."

Secret #11

Vividly Picture a Body Part.

I used to think I was the only oddball who did this, but it turns out that many other women find visualizing body parts extra stimulating too. I usually imagine a close-up view of my breasts, nipples extended and quivering. Somehow this heightens their sensitivity and sends intense orgasm signals to my vagina. Other sensual visualizers share their secrets: "I get an image of what my clitoris must look like to a man, from a straight-on view. It seems huge, red, and wet. Then if I just touch it with my fingertip, I have an orgasm immediately." "I see my vaginal walls swelling and filling with blood, and the back of my vagina opening up to accommodate this huge dildo I have. I see the dildo in there, too, thrusting against the walls and forcing them to open even more. The power of this image really gets me, for some reason, and I then imagine I'm actually watching the spasms of these swollen walls as they release all the energy they've been holding."

Secret #12

Keep Your Rhythm and Pressure Steady.

This is a biggie. Almost every woman I know says the trouble with trying to have an orgasm with a man is that he's likely to change the exquisite thing he's doing to you just when you've reached a level of unbearable sexual tension. At that point, it's crucial to *not change a thing*. "Yes!" a friend of mine agreed. "It must be exactly the same rhythm, motion, pressure, speed, everything for the last twenty or thirty seconds. If not, the whole thing is ruined!" Another smart lady capitalizes on this essential element: "After I come, I just keep up the same steady, hard stimulation even though at first it feels like I can't stand to be touched. Pretty soon that intensity goes away and I just keep on riding the waves of pleasure into multiple-orgasmic bliss."

Secret #13

Tease Yourself.

You can intensify and prolong your orgasm by building tension to a peak but stopping before you go over the edge. Lighten your touch or move to a different area while the level of arousal drops, then rises again. The more times you do this, the greater will be your release in the end. "I love to tease myself into a powerful orgasm by moving my vibrator down from my clit to my vaginal opening when I'm almost ready to come. I hold it there for a while and hang suspended until all pulse stops racing and then move it back to my clit," my friend Joan said. "I do this about ten

times before I finally let myself come; then I just explode."
Another shameless self-tease confesses, "If I take my time,
build up slowly, then let myself come down again, maybe
just rubbing my breasts between peaks, I get this almost
unbearable feeling of wanting to jump out of my skin after
about five times."

Secret #14

Experiment with Breathing Patterns.

Every woman seems to have a different way of using her
breath to enhance her orgasmic capabilities. Explore your
breathing repertoire until you find just the right lung action for you. "I make sure that I have an orgasm every day,
because it helps relieve the stress of my high-power job," a
colleague told me. "I find that breathing deeply is very important for me, no matter what I'm doing, but especially
when I'm pleasuring myself. I just breathe very deeply and
imagine that the air is being breathed in and out of my vagina. It seems to make my insides tingle just enough to
bring me off beautifully."

Other heavy breathers say: "I've found that if I hold
my breath, it helps me over the plateau." "Panting in short,
rhythmic gasps really increases the sensation in my whole
vulval area and makes me come faster. In fact, if I keep up
these pants after my first orgasm and rub myself more

gently, the hypersensitivity in my clit disappears and I can go into another sexual buildup and another orgasm—even five or six more."

Secret #15

Make Sounds.

Withholding noises can stifle your orgasmic feelings, while letting them out frees you to express what you feel inside. Here's what several vocal women have to say: "If I don't scream like a banshee, I can't come." "When I moan, I get more into my feelings. I don't know if I could have an orgasm without letting these sexual urges out." "I actually talk to myself about how sexy I look and how good it feels. I say things I would tell a man, like, 'Ooooo, it feels so good when you suck my tits.' It makes me really hot, and then I just can't keep from coming."

Secret #16

Change or Combine Types of Stimulation.

Once you have an orgasm, try changing your type or place of stimulation to encourage another one. Or combine several styles at once. One voracious lady says, "My first orgasm comes from fingering my clitoris. But my second one usually arrives only if I plunge a dildo real deep into my vagina and pump it hard."

Many women say that if they simply change positions, with their fingers or vibrator approaching from a different angle, they can induce more orgasms. Another woman gluttonous for pleasure says, "After I come once, I just add on another erogenous zone. I keep my fingers in my vagina, but also rub my bottom or twirl my nipples to make more climaxes."

Secret # 17

Push.

Bearing down or pushing seems to trigger orgasm for many women. Sara says, "When I want to have an orgasm, I just push down, as I did when I had my baby. The extra pressure sends me flying." Another multiply orgasmic lady says, "After my first climax, my clitoris is less responsive to touch, so I create more sensation by pushing hard against my fingers to bring on another one." And another affirms, "Bearing down on the dildo makes all my inner skin feel exposed and extra-sensitive. I come right away like that, several times."

Secret #18

Learn to Distinguish Between Clitoral and Vaginal Orgasms.

Vaginal orgasms are quite different from clitoral ones, and you may not realize you're having one because your contractions are not the intense muscular spasms of clitoral climax but the deeper, more oceanlike waves of vaginal orgasm, and this may set you on an orgasmic plateau that leads to other things.

"When I have a vaginal orgasm, my whole pelvis, and sometimes my entire body, bounces and shakes," Rachel explained. "It happens when I use my dildo to rub the very back of my uterus, deep inside. After one of these, I'm satisfied, but then I crave lots more sex, mainly with a real live cock. So my husband loves it when I please myself this way." One vibrating vixen says, "I love to make my clit come first with Jerry the Vibrator. Then I set him aside and use my fingers to caress just inside my vulva until it starts undulating inside. Then if I touch my G-spot, this delicious liquid starts flowing that feels like it comes from the middle of my being."

Secret #19

Ride Your State of Mind Beyond Orgasm.

One cosmic seductress shared these provocative thoughts on going beyond orgasm: "To me, orgasm is like the electric charge of putting your finger in a socket—an exciting feeling but a little crude. I find that if I get my head out of the way, feel completely safe, and let go of all my inhibitions and fears, I can go beyond that violent charge into a delicious hum, a state of bliss that can go on for quite a long time. When I'm completely in touch with my Inner Sex Goddess, she knows what to do with my body and leads the way. But you have to be willing to unite completely—not with a partner but with yourself."

The Taoist masters, too, have always regarded the feeling of oneness achieved during and following orgasmic ecstasy as the most easily accessible mystical experience. So if you approach pleasuring and orgasm not just as a physical release but as a spiritual adventure, you too may find that a mystical place even beyond orgasm lies deliciously within your self-loving grasp.

9

cleopatra's pleasure toys— electric, plastic, furry, and human

althougth it is said that, on many nights, Cleopatra would summon hundreds of her soldiers to take their individual turn satisfying and being satisfied by her seemingly endless capacity for sexual pleasuring, once she met Mark Antony she became a one-man woman. And while he was off fighting wars and acquiring new territory for their kingdom, she would slake her robust sexual appetite with a wide assortment of inventive and luxurious toys, from dildos fashioned of smooth wood or stone to gold-chain pleasure halters, papyrus reed ticklers, and carefully selected clusters of grapes. Aside from quenching a queen's lusty thirst, Cleopatra's pleasure toys also kept the jewel of her libido sparkling, piqued and developed her prodigious imagination, and enhanced her magnetically irresistible sex appeal. Her eyes literally smoldered with passionate invitation when Antony returned from campaigning, and she wantonly initiated him into whatever new and secret seductions she had invented during their long separation. She was a woman profoundly in touch with her Inner Sex Goddess.

As a queen, Cleopatra knew that gold and land were her most necessary allies. But as a woman, she believed that a finely carved dildo was truly a girl's best friend.

Much more charming and fun companions on a solitary evening, they're much more affordable and easier to procure too. Today's vibrating dildos and modern pulsing massagers provide a reliable source of high orgasmic pleasure that can't be beat—in fact, using a vibrator is how I discovered what an orgasm was in the first place. My friend Sally says she used to need an hour and a half of hand stimulation before she could have an orgasm, but with her trusty electric toy she can reach a shuddering climax in ten minutes or less if she wants to. Joan, a very focused and intense woman in her frisky sixties, reports that she needs up to two hours of rapid pulsation directly on her clitoris to reach her peak. For her, a vibrator provides the consistent, long-lasting stimulation her body wants and needs but that neither she nor her husband has the stamina to maintain by hand. Well-known sex therapist Pauline Abrams says, "It takes longer for me to come with a vibrator, because I can't control the feedback system as well as with my own hand," but most women find that the concentrated, unflagging stimulation provided by an electric pleasure toy makes for easier, faster, and often more intense orgasms than they can count on with any other method.

A vibrator works by quivering and shaking the millions of nerve endings in the skin of your genitals. It can trigger at least a million more sensors than the most skillful hand or penis, meaning that an intensely high level of arousal, if not ecstatic orgasm, is inevitable. But don't worry that you'll become addicted. In fact, quite the opposite is usually the case. Most women find that when they learn the full extent of their erotic capacity by self-pleasuring with vibrators and other sex toys, they are at last able to transfer these satiating talents and sensations to other styles of lovemaking, whether on their own or with their partners.

Just like sex goddesses, vibrators come in many styles, shapes, and sizes. Like me, you may choose to acquire an entire inventory of vibrating toys to suit your different sensual moods. Or, like Joan, you may prefer the simplicity of one perfect pleasure wand, always impeccably attuned to your particular cravings. Whichever your predilection, you can buy most types of vibrators in an ordinary drugstore because they are basically massagers for the whole body. For other types, such as dildo vibrators, you may need to visit your local sex store or browse through the many tasteful sex toy catalogs currently available. Once acquired, you can prolong your vibrator's life and the quality of service it gives you by storing it in a cool, dry place—I keep mine in a cloth bag, snuggled in a drawer—and wiping it clean after every use with a cloth moistened with warm water or alcohol. Never immerse your vibrator-massager in water.

swedish-style scalp massagers

Held on by straps around the palm, these massagers are small vibrating boxes that sit on the back of your hand. They make your whole hand vibrate gently. Although the pulsations they produce are not as intense as wand or coil-operated vibrators, the advantage of Swedish-style massagers is the skin-to-skin contact they permit and the versatility of being able to transport vibrations to any body area that your eager hand and fingers can reach. So for a lovely silky sort of vibratory experience, strap on your Swedish massager and make your hand flow sensually over your body like that of one of Cleopatra's handmaidens in the milk bath.

133. Glide over your entire body with your electrified hand, delving into every crevice and cranny with this quivering sensation. When you vibrate your skin, you stimulate the flow of blood to that area, a marvelous health and beauty treatment for the entire body. And you will discover that areas previously not so erotically sensitive will awaken to new sensual thrills at your vibrating touch — your scalp, lower back, fingers, and toes, for example. So skate lightly over the skin, hold firmly in one spot, or massage as you go. Tingle your soft lips, earlobes, and nipples. Massage your tummy and inner thighs. Tickle the bottoms of your feet, your inner elbows, and the curve of your fanny. Try performing the Mirror of Sensual Transformation ritual with a vibrating hand and see how marvelously different it feels.

134. Vibrate your vulva. Cup your entire pubic mound in your pulsating palm; slowly press in and feel the deep waves ripple throughout your entire body. Let your fingers rest lightly on your clitoris and vaginal lips. Massage your rosebud and moist vaginal opening with your softly buzzing hand. Squeeze them gently. Insert one vibrating fingertip inside your vagina. Just hold it there while you tingle; then rotate it and slide it in and out. Sneak up on your G-spot and make it throb. With your new quivering touch, you can add a fresh dimension to what you did in numbers 35 through 132.

135. If you didn't become an immediate fan of anal self-play in Chapter 4, try it with your *electrified* fingers. You may discover, as did my friend Sharon, that the delicate tissues there, richly endowed with sensual nerve endings, literally invite vibrations. She says, "I love to strap on my Swedish massager and lay the tip of my middle finger against the opening in my behind. The vibrations feel

sooooo good, and somehow primal. At the same time I rub my clit and labia with the other hand. It's kind of like being rocked in an unbelievably sexy cradle."

electric wand and coil-operated vibrators

As used by most modern sex goddesses, these vibrators are great for super stimulation of the genital area, especially the clitoris, thereby quickly propelling you into the blissful throes of first-time orgasms, nectar-producing orgasms, and even multiple orgasms. As such, they are highly recommended by Aphrodite, the Cloud Damsels, the sensual descendants of Cleopatra, and 99.7 percent of all Inner Sex Goddesses as an especially fine way to develop deep communion with them. And the more you express your Inner Sex Goddess self, the deeper and more electric is your communion with your lover. So pick out the vibrator type best suited to you, and aim for the stars.

A wand vibrator is composed of a tennis-ball-sized vibrating head attached to a foot-long phallic handle. One of the oldest and most popular types, this magic wand generates a strong penetrating vibration, diffused over the rounded rubber head, and it's very easy to maneuver. It can be easily stationed between you and your lover, providing both of you with powerful vibes and free hands.

Coil-operated vibrators have smaller handles, usually about seven inches long, and a vibrating metal plug on the side to which you can fasten a fun assortment of vinyl attachments—rounded, pronged, and cuplike. They generate more focused, super-fast vibrations, are relatively lightweight and quiet, and have the advantage of variety over the vibrating head. Both wand and coil-operated vibrators usually have two speeds of operation, which basically translate to "intense" and *really* intense." So handle these toys with care, but do handle them.

136. Since wand and coil-operated vibrators were really made to be body massagers, you can and should use them to voluptuously tingle the skin all over your body. Employ the longer wand vibrators to pleasure places you can't normally reach with your hands. Massage the middle of your back, for instance, while you twirl your nipples with your free hand, or extend the wand down to tickle the bottoms of both feet while you rub your clitoris with your free hand. Play with the attachments of a coil-operated model on different parts of your body—perhaps the suction cup over a toe, the pronged number to scratch your back, or the small rounded one to slip into your navel. Or simply give yourself an all-over vibrating massage before you move on to more sexual endeavors.

137. Although the possible combinations of body parts and vibrator attachments are tantalizingly endless, here are some suggestions for each tingling attachment that Cleopatra would have loved to have in her collection. The dome of the suction cup is perfect for crowning your clitoris with euphoric pulsations; it fits over and around your little Jewel of the Nile without touching it directly. Try using the pronged attachment to simulate the grazing of Mark Antony's teeth on your milk-wet nipples. The small rounded tip is excellent for penetrating *in* to sensitive places, like a smoothed Nile pebble having an earthquake inside your moist interior caves. And the ringed diffuser spreads the tantalizing tingles over the fleshy mounds of your honeyed breast or your jasmine-perfumed pubis; and, if pressed down firmly, it sends caressing pulsations deep into your very bones.

138. Nipples and vibrators go well together. The round ball of a wand vibrator can impart a wonderful tingly feeling when smoothed over or pressed deep into a rosy areola. Cupping a nipple with the domed attachment of a coil-operated model might remind you of a small, sucking mouth. For a sharper, more intense sensation, pass either the pronged or the spot massager lightly over your nipples; this can send darts of excitement to your lower regions, warming them up for further self-play.

139. When you feel ready to move the vibrator to your genitals, you may want to soften the intensity of its pulsations at first. Too strong a pressure or movement can kill your building passion. Try placing a folded towel, a pillow, or a piece of clothing, like maybe your sexy panties or teddy, between your delicate vaginal or clitoral tissues and the head of the vibrator. Or encase the whole vibrator in a thick cotton sock. This will help diffuse the vibrations, and the different texture against your skin will add a thrill all its own.

140. Massage your outer and inner love lips with the vibrator. Long, slow strokes bring out the best and hottest levels of sensation. At some point stop and hold the head maddeningly steady against your urethral opening or your vaginal opening. Let the constant, steady pulsations melt into you and spread a throbbing glow throughout your whole body.

141. You know how maddeningly exciting it is when your lover teases you by completely removing his penis from your vulva, pausing, and then resuming his amorous assault. Do the same with your vibrator by continually raising it away from your body and bringing it back again.

142. Try inserting your stone egg (from the PC muscle exercises) or some ben wa balls into your vagina and then holding the vibrator against your vaginal opening. The egg or balls will rattle around deliciously.

143. One sexy editor I know says she likes to rest a finger on her clitoris and then vibrate her finger with the rim of the suction cup attachment. Of course, this finger arrangement can also travel farther down across your inner lips to create a throbbing vulval massage.

144. Though this is a delicate undertaking, most women use their vibrators to bestow otherwise impossible raptures upon their yearning clits. Techniques for doing this are as varied as the women who invent and relish them. Some stir their wands over and around the clitoral tip in slow, lazy circles. Others rub up and down or back and forth. They may alternate these movements with simply holding the vibrator lightly in place or rhythmically pulsing it in and out like a slow, gentle love tap. One young and blissfully married swim instructor I know says she prefers to plant her vibrator firmly over her clitoris and then very slowly increase the urgency by pressing it in closer and closer until the vibrator is mushing her clitoris into her pubic mound and the entire area is throbbing wildly. Then she switches the vibrator control to high!

145. While vibrating your clitoris in the manner of your choice, trail your moistened fingers over the soft fur-

row between your labia, circle around your vaginal opening, and slip inside. Rotate, tickle, or thrust appropriately.

146. A favored method of my friend Beverly, a bookish professor of philosophy, is to vibrate her clitoris while manually massaging her nipples, and then alternate with the opposite procedure—vibrating her trembling tips while manually massaging her love bud. For Beverly, as for many women, there is a direct and powerful connection between these two hot spots that is electrified by the simultaneous pulsing and pulling actions. She says it's a great turn-on for her to watch this in the mirror too—as it would be for any lucky lover, by the way.

147. You can simulate the skin-to-skin pulsations of a Swedish scalp massager by resting your wand or coil-operated vibrator on the back of your hand as you stroke, knead, and slap with your fingers or palm. With a little imagination, these strokes could feel like the delicious ministrations of your man's mouth, hand, or "sacred snake."

148. Insert a fingertip to pinpoint your G-spot and then vibrate it by placing your magic wand on the part of your finger, knuckle, or hand that remains outside.

149. My next-door neighbor, an avid sensualist, suggests laying your vibrator, head up, on a pillow, kneeling or squatting over it, and touching your genitals to its pulsing head as lightly or firmly, as fast or slow, as you desire. Pump your hips, à la Elvis, over the humming surface.

150. Free your hands for erotic self-exploration by creatively engineering a harness to hold your vibrator in place against your labia or clitoris. Tie a long scarf under your pelvis and vibrator, and over your shoulder. Two scarves crisscrossed around your hips can work even better. Or don the bottom half of your bikini swimsuit and insert the vibrator head between cloth and skin.

151. I've found that if you hold the vibrator lightly against your love bud and use the middle finger of your other hand to tickle and caress the outside of your vaginal opening and the area just inside it, the voluptuous sensations and images of a lover's penis rubbing against your moist vulva are magically and meltingly evoked.

152. One day over crullers and coffee my friend Marion confessed to me, "I love to rent steamy sex videos and watch them with a vibrator in my lap. I copy everything they do in the movie, whether it involves somebody's hand or tongue or even a man's penis, except that I'm doing it with my vibrator. I rub it all over my face, breasts, genitals, and derriere. Whatever they do, I get turned on by watching it and feeling my own vibrations at the same time." A great way to double your pleasure!

153. Using either a wand vibrator or one of the smooth attachments on a coil-operated vibrator, slip the oscillating head around to your anal opening and massage gently. Don't try to insert it. With your free hand, rub your swollen labia and/or clitoris. Close your eyes and float on a dreamy, cradling cloud, or imagine your lover's tongue there.

154. Even though your vibrator is a wonderfully powerful love machine, don't make it do all the work. Move your body against it, gyrate your hips, swivel your fanny into it, undulate over and around its pulsing head. From a prone position with knees bent, thrust your pelvis up off the bed, tighten your tummy and PC muscle, and grind against the massager. Kneel or stand with legs outstretched and do the lambada or the limbo with your mechanical partner. Bend over and slip the vibrator between your legs to massage your tender thighs and labial mound; grip it with your thighs and squeeze, as if it's another phallus you know and love.

155. Get personal. Plenty of women have told me they have pet names for their vibrators—Sam, Vic the Vibrator, Thor (the god of thunder!), Valentino, Reginald Rutabaga III, and so on. The woman who dubbed her vibrator Valentino often plays flamenco music and wears one of those black gaucho hats with a chin strap when she has a rendezvous with her electrically powered lover.

156. Many sex toy shops and mail-order catalogs carry a variety of vibrator attachments specifically designed for sexual use—including "cliticklers" (perfect for focusing vibrations on one spot) and G-spotters (curved to tuck against your labia or to insert for vaginal vibration). There's even one shaped like a two-pronged twig that tingles your clitoris and your inner vaginal walls simultaneously or pulsates deliciously inside your anus. Sometimes half the fun of these attachments is shopping for them in the first place and imagining the dazzling variety of uses to which you can put them. So don't be too shy to indulge in this harmlessly pleasurable pursuit—or to actually cavort with these naughty little toys either!

157. Okay, say your vibrator has brought you to a thrilling orgasmic peak, and say your love bud is now supersensitive and shy of further vibratory touch, so you think the fun is over. Only your Inner Sex Goddess knows for sure, but you could probably go on to several more orgasms and reach places in your deep, hot sexuality you never knew existed. If you simply relax, take a few deep belly breaths, and let your hand rest between the vibe and you while you gently rotate against it, you can sustain the lovely orgasmic plateau and allow your clitoris to rejuvenate itself for further, heightened responses. This is when your Inner Sex Goddess *really* comes alive.

dildos and battery vibrators

Derived from the Italian word *diletto*, which means "delight," dildos are penislike objects used for delightful sensual pleasuring. Battery-operated vibrators are simply dildos that vibrate. Since you do basically the same things with both devices, I've lumped them together here for convenience — after all, it's their penislike quality that matters.

And that's of course what mattered to Cleopatra when she had her wood and stone dildos especially carved to order. We don't know for sure, but since clay dildos were found in Egyptian tombs around that same time, we can only imagine what elaborate pleasure wands the Queen of the Nile might have had prepared for her eternal resting place. We do know that Cleopatra treasured her phallic possessions as practical magic for keeping her ripe, vitalizing sensuality within easy reach. The Egyptian temptress intuitively understood that sense memories are stored all over the body, and the touch of phallus to vulva can spark off internal nerve messages that evoke lust and love.

Throughout the ages, people of all cultures have unabashedly used carved phalluses as delightful keys to unlock deep sexual feelings. The people of ancient times actually considered dildos sacred. Originally worshiped as fertility gods, they were believed to house the magical potency of life itself. In India, holy lingams made of stone, metal, or ivory, representing the god Siva, were used to deflower virgins as a sacred rite of passage before marriage. And in ancient Rome, it was a statue of the phallus god Mutunus Tutunus who presented his staggering equipment for affianced young girls to ceremonially straddle.

In ancient Japan and China, a wife would often have a replica of her husband's penis made of tortoiseshell, horn, or wood, with his name beautifully inscribed on it. Greatly cared for and kept in a specially made box, it was a much-venerated likeness of his actual form that could be doted upon and used for self-satisfaction during the prolonged absence of a loved and loving mate.

In the harems of Arabia and the social and sacred events of Greece, dildos continued to develop new and more interesting forms, and around A.D. 500 a nice touch was added: dildos began to be made from sealing wax so they would absorb body heat. By the 1100s, the clever French had invented long red rubber instruments called *consolateurs* that held milk or other liquids that could be pumped out to simulate ejaculation.

Today both vibrating and nonvibrating dildos come in an astonishing variety of shapes, sizes, and colors, perfect for each libidinous lady and her every sensual mood. Vibrating dildos made from plastic, vinyl, or rubber are relatively inexpensive and portable, and they produce vibrations gentler than the wand or coil-operated vibrators. Some are plain hard cylinders while others approximate the softer feel and luscious look of a real penis. Take your pick. I have a delightfully mischievous friend who loves to give the plain cylindrical kind—not very lifelike, but effective—as first-time vibrator gifts. Wearing a catlike grin, she told me, "They're nonthreatening, affordable, and always appreciated."

Regular dildos are equally insertable, portable, and affordable—they just don't vibrate. What they do is provide a delicious feeling of fullness in the vagina (or rectum); the movement is up to you. They too are made from rubber or plastic, but some are fashioned from a very lifelike silicone, and some even sport little protrusions that look and feel like testicles.

Because they come in a wide variety of shapes, sizes, and colors, buying a regular or a vibrating dildo can be a mind-boggling experience. I've seen them as small as 4 1/4 inches long and an inch in diameter, and as big as 10 inches long by 2 1/4 inches. They come in every color, from flesh to black to turquoise, and in shapes ranging from plain cylinders to ducks, whales, and dolphins to lifelike models of a famous porn star's equipment. Relying on your own personal tastes, you shouldn't have too much trouble selecting a color and shape to suit you, but size can be deceiving. Some women choose a dildo too small because they underestimate the expanded scope of an aroused vagina, while others find that their eyes are much bigger than their sexual appetites. I recommend experimenting with vegetables first—zucchini, cucumbers, and carrots—to determine the perfect fit for you. Then let your Inner Sex Goddess be your guide.

158. First things first. Always lubricate your dildo before use because, far from being innately slippery, rubber and plastic can be somewhat sticky and can even pinch or abrade your sensitive tissues. But the oiling-up process can be a scintillating project in itself. Like Cleopatra, you might want to wet your dildo with your mouth by sucking on it lustily, as you would your man's penis. When I attended a class in the art of fellatio, I was delighted to discover that the instructor actually got turned on by using a lifelike rubber dildo to demonstrate oral technique. This practice is not at all weird or perverted; it's sensual as all

get-out. In fact, I often have hot oral sex with my dildo while I pleasure myself in other ways at the same time. Try it. The other lubing option is to rub your dildo with oil in the same sensuous way you would massage your lover's equipment. Again, with a little imagination, this procedure can be an entrancing turn-on for you.

159. Asking what women like to do with dildos is like asking "What do women want?" Basically, everything. Your repertoire should be limited only by your imagination. With your vibrating dildo, try everything you like to do with your regular vibrator. Use your nonvibrating dildo to perform some version of whatever you enjoy doing with your hands and fingers. Make either kind do all the lovely things to you that your man's love tool does, and all the things you *wish* it could do. It's your dream penis to do with—and be done unto with—as you please. Look at it. Fondle it. Lick it. Screw it. Make it last for hours. Experiment with wild new ways of making love that you can shock your lucky man with later.

160. Here's what my friend Charlene, a freckled, fresh-faced mom, likes to do: "First I smooth the oiled head of my dildo up and down my vaginal lips. Then I press it in a little deeper so it snuggles in between them. Still moving it forward and back, I bring the dildo up to massage my clitoris, then down to nuzzle it barely inside

my opening—just enough so that the lip of the dildo head catches on the rim of my vagina. After I pull it in and out a few times, I start the whole routine over again, keeping myself from pushing the entire length deep inside as long as I can—because as soon as I do, I have the most fantastic orgasm."

161. Create a welcoming space for your dildo by fingering your clitoris long enough to get your juices flowing. Still massaging your delicate rosebud, dip the dildo into your musky lubricating fluids and slip it slowly inside you. Then slide it in and out, matching the cadence of your thrusts with your clitoral strokes and firing off all those lovely inner sex neurons. Keeping the two motions going, quicken your pace until you are thrusting and rubbing at lightning speed. See how far out into the galaxy you can take yourself.

162. As you are thrusting, you might want to get your PC muscle into the rhythm too, squeezing it around the plunging dildo so that you can feel its texture against your sensitive vaginal walls. Remember that contracting your inner muscles also pulls on your clitoris, so you'll get a double whammy effect with these sensations. And it's great practice for milking your man's hot member.

163. Try inserting your dildo as deep as possible and just holding it there. If it's a vibrator, flick on the switch after it's in place and let the vibrations radiate throughout your entire vaginal cavity. With a nonvibrating dildo, just focus on the luscious feeling of fullness. Let your other hand caress your body erotically as you fashion day-dreams of cradling the love-swollen penis of the sexiest man alive.

164. I know a woman who prefers to insert her dildo at oblique angles so that it stretches and pulls at her vaginal opening yet penetrates very little. She says, "This way, it hits all those special spots, inside and out, that drive me crazy, and I feel always on the edge, craving more."

165. Many women like to alternate deep, powerful plunges that pound into the inner recesses of their love cave with shallow, almost playful thrusts that excite the tighter entryway section. You can even let the dildo slip out completely sometimes, experiencing a lovely tug against your inner lips and vaginal rim each time you rein-sert it. Show your lover how to do this with his flesh-and-blood phallus.

166. Experiment with varying leg positions to achieve different effects: knees together or spread wide; sitting, reclining, or kneeling; standing in front of a full-length mirror; on your side with legs drawn up; on all fours; in a chair with your legs draped over the arms; face down while imagining being taken by a Mongol warrior. My manicurist says she likes to half recline with one knee up and the other flat on the bed. Then she brings her dildo in from behind, leaving plenty of room for the other hand to massage her clitoris or outer lips. This also brings the tip of the dildo in contact with the front wall of her vagina, where she undoubtedly has a goddess spot or two.

167. A great position, if you can manage it, is lying on your back, knees spread wide, feet together and drawn up close to your bottom. Hold the dildo inside you and maneuver it with your feet. All the muscles around your vagina and its lips are being stimulated by the stretch of your legs as well as the exertions of your feet. And this lightly athletic marvel leaves both hands free for erotic exploration to your nipples and clitoris or other erotic venues. If there were a Sexual Olympics, this would surely be a hotly contested event!

168. If you have a dildo with a suction cup base, try sticking it to the floor; then squat over it with legs spread wide and bounce up and down wildly. You can create very deep penetration and play with your breasts at the same time. Do your man the biggest favor of his life and let him watch you next time.

169. Mary Ann, whose husband is often away scouting locations, has become quite chummy with her vibrating dildo. She says it makes her even hotter for Bill when she stretches her love lips wide open with the fingers of one hand and plunges her dildo in and out with the other. She comments, "Not only does this feel great and remind me of my lover, but it's incredible to watch in the mirror too."

170. As you tease, thrust, and rub with your dildo, letting yourself get more and more rapidly out of control, you may find it amusing to deliberately slow the pace by plunging your dildo in as deep as possible and just letting it rest there. Massage your clitoris very languidly and gently until your breathing is back to normal. Then speed up again, bringing yourself to a peak three or four times before you finally let the overpowering spasms carry you over the edge.

171. Sex therapist Pauline Abrams says, "I have my best orgasms if I put a dildo inside me so that it touches my cervix and then use the vibrator. That makes my orgasms much stronger." You can use the vibrator to steam up your clitoris and, while doing slow, sensuous penetration, gyrate on the dildo and vibrator at the same time. Or occasionally move the vibrator to the base of the dildo to send fiery pulsations rocketing up inside you. Another idea is to hold the dildo inside you by squeezing your legs together so that one hand is free for the vibrator and the other is available to tease your nipples or to perform some other delight.

172. Insert your dildo about halfway and revolve it around and around the neck of your womb as if you were stirring up a delicious batter of passion cookies. This is especially intoxicating when done with a vibrating dildo turned up to full speed.

173. Adorn your dildo with a ribbed or contoured condom to create a subtle but stimulating variation on the sensations it produces. It's a great way to practice safe fantasy sex with your favorite outrageously endowed porn star.

174. Accessorize. Don a hat, scarf, gloves, shirt pulled open to expose your breasts, garter belt, and stockings under a tight dress, earrings in your pubic hair, temporary tattoos—anything you might not feel brazen enough to wear for your lover. The sight of yourself in the mirror, coquettishly attired, with a lovely plump phallus sliding in and out of you, may give you the salacious ideas you've always wished you had.

175. For a delightful tease, skim a vibrating dildo back and forth over your perineum for five to ten minutes before allowing yourself to push it into the deep well of your vagina.

176. In some sex toy stores and catalogs, you can purchase hollow dildos containing a rubber or latex tube that's open at one end. You fill the tube with warm water or cream, or take a tip from the Italians and use egg whites or even fish eggs. Then you thrust the dildo in and out in your favorite manner and eject your fantasy lover's "vital essence" at the moment of your climax.

177. Though this may be not to everyone's taste, I just have to pass along what seems like an exotically stimulating idea from a very adventurous friend of mine. Says she, "I like that vibrating feeling in my behind; it seems to go all the way up through my vagina and stomach. That's why I often slide my vibrator dildo gently into my rear and smooth my fingers around the stretched opening there. Usually I just lie back and let the feeling build, but sometimes I play with my clitoris or the inside of my vagina. If I slip my fingers inside, I can feel the vibrations through the skin of my vagina, especially if I twirl the vibrator dildo around in that direction. It's a real deep, earthy sensation that makes me shudder and shake like a volcano."

178. And here's one more from yet another lusty adventuress: "I think two dildos are better than one, and I

like to come up with creative ways to use both my small penislike vibrator and my big lifelike dildo. First I make the little one slippery by sliding it into my cozy slit. Then I slip it into the hole in my bottom and switch it on. Next I glide my Superman-size dildo ever so slowly into my vagina, push it in and out, and churn it around in circles. I imagine that some burly, sweaty construction worker is having his way with me and being real rough. This somehow blasts all my inhibitions right out of the water, and I pound against him like a wild woman. And once I've got all that going, I still have one hand free to stroke my clit. I haven't yet tried using another vibrator for my clitoris, but that's next on my list!"

cleo's grab bag

With the power, ingenuity, and resources to have any sensual toy imaginable created for her, the precocious Queen of the Nile collected quite a cache of inventive pleasuring instruments. But her favorites were always her dildos and the simple little things like ibis feathers, lion fur, and of course milk baths. These pleasures she indulged in for both solo and partner lovemaking. While vibrators and dildos are at the top of almost every modern Sex Goddess's toy list, there is a veritable cornucopia of other scintillating playthings you too can use to coax delectable pleasures from your silky, sexy body—and that of your lover. Though some of the suggestions that follow may bend the boundaries of your self-pleasuring comfort zone, put on your sultry Cleopatra crown and let her try them out for you. You may be surprised at your exotically expanded capacity for pleasure.

179. Ancient Indian texts suggest that natural substances make the best penetration toys; they recommend radishes, mangoes, and gourds as well as the usual bananas, carrots, cucumbers, and zucchini. (One zany advertising writer says, "Thank God for zucchini—it has ridges! But I always practice safe vegetable sex and use condoms to avoid contact with pesticides.") Fascinatingly, the ancients also suggested a "reed made soft with oil" and the stalk of a plant which, when soaked in hot water, swells up and takes on an "agreeable warmth and texture." Mmm, sounds yummy. Of course, if they were around today they might also advocate using pickles (with their titillating knobs and crevices), Popsicles (deliciously icy, and fun to eat afterward), corn on the cob (lube it well first!), or even hot dogs (wet, slippery, flexible, cold, and sort of lifelike in color). Consult your Inner Sex Goddess on any richly inventive ideas she may have.

$180.$ An artist friend of mine suggests sculpting your vegetable of choice to size, or to an interesting shape, with a potato parer, leaving enough skin at the bottom so it won't slip out of your fervid grasp. She says she goes into another world when she puts on her headphones, inserts her artistically molded eggplant, and lets her regular vibrator tickle her clitoris unmercifully. When designing your vegetable penis, don't trim too close to the center or it will go limp.

$181.$ Almost any smooth object shaped like a cylinder can be used as a dildo—like candles, for instance. Just remember that your internal tissues are delicate; so don't use anything that's glass or metal or that has rough edges or sharp corners. Be as discriminating about your stand-in lovers as you are about your flesh-and-blood men.

$182.$ Ben wa balls can provide an exhilarating internal massage, especially if you activate them with a vibrator (as suggested in 142) or by walking, dancing, or exercising while they jiggle around. These are especially handy for an ultimately unattainable fantasy—having a man's penis massaging your vaginal walls all day. You could also insert a vibrating dildo in your bottom and point it toward the ben wa balls just on the other side of the sensitive dividing tissues.

183. The Japanese have a slightly different version of their own ben wa balls—called rin-no-tama balls. One of these small brass spheres is hollow and the other contains a tiny heavy metal ball or quicksilver, so that the balls constantly roll against each other. You insert them in your vagina—put the empty ball in first—and secure them with a tampon. Any pelvic movement causes them to shimmy around and tickle your insides mercilessly.

184. Most sex toy stores or catalogs carry a little gem of an item called a Kegelcisor. Made of heavy brass, it's a small barbell for exercising your PC muscle (doing Kegel exercises), based on the concept that it's easier to build up strength and tone if you have to work against a resistive device. It's about 6 and 3/4 inches long and has three small spheres, one at either end and one in the middle, that are 1/4 inch to 1 and 1/8 inches in diameter. This fancy fitness tool builds love muscles to grasp your man with, and it can be a uniquely gratifying dildo as well.

185. Ice is a fabulous toy. Rub a frosty ice cube across your nipples, over your vaginal lips and clitoris, and inside the walls of your womb. You may prefer "warm" ice that has been sitting out for some time or the cold shock of ice cubes fresh from the freezer. Place an ice cube inside your vagina and let it melt as you massage your vulva, or use a vibrator on your labia to blend an internal "cherry" daiquiri. You can make a chilling dildo by freezing a cucumber or by very carefully filling an extra-sturdy and/or large condom with water and popping it in the freezer. A few hours later cut away the condom and *voilà!*—an ice penis to play with.

186. A truly marvelous toy for sale at most sex stores is a Venus Butterfly massager. This tiny vibrating pad, which lies over your clitoris and straps on around your thighs, allows you to enjoy continuous titillation on your love bud while your hands are completely free to roam over the rest of your hot bod.

187. Of course, it's good to have some playthings for the rest of your body too. Taking an inventory of the self-pleasuring treasure troves of several sensuous friends (nightstand drawers, shoe boxes under the bed, even safe-deposit boxes), I discovered the following collection of simple little toys kept handy to make the skin tingle all over the body: a small piece of rabbit fur, ostrich and peacock feathers, a feather duster, silk scarves, the satin from a discarded camisole, a lace doily, black leather gloves, a small rubber ball, wool mittens, the ratty pronged attachment from a long-abandoned vibrator, a satin-smooth wooden egg, a collection of thimbles for each fingertip, cloth flowers, a soft cuddly teddy bear, an old woven place mat, elbow-length cotton gloves, part of a beaded car-seat cover, felt squares, a terry washcloth, a large fluffy makeup brush, the ruffle from a taffeta petticoat, pieces of Velcro, and the long Cleopatra wig from an old Halloween costume. Whether you employ these skin-sational toys by your own private self or invite your lover to join in, they provide easy and fun inducements to coax your Inner Sex Goddess out of hiding.

188. Nobody talks about it, but millions of ordinary, virtuous, and sane women find that a little loving bondage provides a hot, intense, and daring addition to their self-pleasuring repertoire. If you've wondered about it but are a little squeamish, self-play can be a wonderfully private, fun, and safe outlet for your budding bondage fantasies—and a special delight for your sizzling Cleopatra-esque personality. While sex toy stores have all kinds of fancy handcuffs, whips, clamps, blindfolds, and chains, there are perfectly wonderful substitutes for all of these wicked toys right in the sanctity of your own palace. Scarves, stockings, bras, and panties make fabulous handcuffs and blindfolds; choker necklaces, ribbons, or long strands of pearls can become decorative slave collars; belts, towels, dustpans, and Ping-Pong paddles can be used for sensuous self-spankings. One friend of mine, who is particularly partial to nipple stimulation, says that clamping her nipples with padded clothespins creates a delicious teasing pinch while leaving her hands free for other delightfully depraved activities. (If you don't have the padded variety, use cotton balls or scarves as a cushion.) Reading a book like *The Story of O* can give you plenty more inventive ideas for playing at submission while providing an erotic state of mind perfect for exploring the sweet tortures of passion.

189. Another unexpected pleasure can come from playing with toys especially made to fit into your bottom. Depending on your personal preferences, you can insert small dildos, carrots, or cucumbers to provide an exquisite feeling of fullness, or larger specially made anal plugs that stretch, and thereby titillate, your tight opening. Anything you insert into your nether regions should be completely smooth and seamless with a flared base to keep it from slipping all the way inside. And always use lots of lubrication. Once your fanny toy is comfortably and safely in place, you have both hands free to roam over other erotic territories. One woman who enjoys euphoric anal sex with her partner told me that, when alone, she likes to circle her fingers around the rim where her rear sex toy emerges while she massages her clitoris with the other hand. Another lusty lady says, "When I really want to come fast, I slide this special rubber plug inside my bottom and then stroke the inside of my vagina with my left hand. This turns my vaginal walls to warm pudding, and the plug makes me feel so wide and extended that my body just opens and comes."

$190.$ Water as a toy offers a fount of sensuous possibilities. Sit in front of the hot, powerful jet stream in a whirlpool bath. Use a bidet, or simply pour warm water over your genitals. Lie in the tub with your vulva directly under the faucet and turn the water on hard, perhaps switching from hot to cold to hot. Remove the head from your shower and let the extra weight of the water falling from a height feel like a thousand tiny fingers rapidly running over your genitals. Marilyn Chambers, star of the classic porn video *Behind the Green Door*, says, "What's really good is a hose in your bathtub. You just die, I swear. Just hook a hose to the faucet and take the spray attachment off. You put it on your clit, then you turn the water up and down—hot or cold—and you go through the ceiling. It's the most wrenching orgasm you will ever have in your life."

$191.$ Then there's a shower massager. The kind you can move around by hand is the only kind to have, of course. Dial the setting to any and every type of spray that takes your fancy—diffuse, pulsing, hard, soft. Wash your inner thighs and navel with hot, tingling liquid. Rub the hard spray directly on your nipples. Spurt pulsing water against your clitoris. Open your labia lips and let the warm liquid pour like cream all over your sensitive membranes. Focus the stream with your hand, and finger yourself within the gushing current. Let hot pulses cascade down the cleavage of your bottom. Spray your entire genital area at different angles and from varying distances, in circles, in long sensuous strokes. Shake it over your throbbing bud and thrust the massager rapidly closer and farther away from your body. Let your Inner Sex Goddess splash around like a wild creature of the deep.

192. I'll bet you've never thought of your douching equipment as a toy, but many women have told me they find it extra-stimulating to pleasure themselves while douching. They say the warm water spraying inside and then dripping over their fingers as they rub their clitoris drenches them in ecstasy—and makes them think of penises bursting with love juice. Even if you don't wish to partake of this watery rapture, you can always use the dry attachments as delightfully different dildos.

193. Brightly colored ribbons, small soft flowers, and decorative hair combs can be used to adorn your pubic hair as a playful masterpiece of sensual art. If you want to go a little further, try shaving your genitalia (an erotic sensation in itself), admiring your innocently exposed elegance, and then applying a pretty, feminine temporary tattoo. Follow up these aesthetics with master strokes of pleasuring massage to your decorated pubis. Reveal your artwork to your man, if you dare.

10

the
goddess
with her
consort

ℵow that you've awakened all the erotic centers of your body and mind and learned to bring yourself via a thousand different paths to the highest peaks of sexual ecstasy, it's time to invite your consort into the game. Of course you've been making love to your man all along, and he's been reaping the benefits of your rapidly developing Sex Goddesshood, but have you shared your hottest autoerotic expertise and passion with him? Have you, for instance, thought about tying up your partner and making him watch while you undulate, shiver, and throb to your own inner rhythms? Well, if not, now's the time to knock his socks off.

Goddess vamp that you are, however, even you may at first feel a little shy about revealing your intimate moves and feelings so boldly. But there are several good reasons for overcoming any lingering bashfulness.

Reason # 1. According to recent research, many couples have their best sex when they engage in self-pleasuring or mutual self-pleasuring prior to or during intercourse. It adds variety (a crucial element in any long-term relationship), spice, mutual trust, and vulnerability, and it deepens intimacy immeasurably. In *The Art of Sensual Loving,* Dr.

Andrew Stanway says, "The value of masturbation cannot be overestimated in any loving relationship."

Reason #2. You can turn your lover's flame up to extra hot with a simple twist of your nipple or stroke of your sexual triangle. Why do you think there's so much female masturbation seen in X-rated videos? Because men are intensely visual and begin to drool helplessly at the sight of a woman in the throes of her own passion. The fact that you are lusty and confident enough to allow him this intimate and thrilling sight of *you* is extra frosting on his erotic cake. A man once told me, "When a woman takes on the full power of her sexuality by loving her own body, and *lets me see it,* she empowers me to be my sexiest self and takes us to places neither one of us has been before."

Reason #3. It takes the passivity out of being the receiving partner. Even in partner sex, you must still be responsible for your own passion, arousal, and orgasmic pleasure. So it's fortifying to know that instead of simply having to respond and follow where your man leads, you can add some flashy steps of your own. And through some magical process of sexual osmosis, it turns out that taking the turns *you* like makes the dance much more exciting for both of you.

Reason #4. It's the best way for your man to learn your sexual needs and desires. You can show him, for example, that when you are touched lightly your body reaches out for more sensation, and that it contracts away if pressed too hard. You can let him see that when your nipples are twirled at just the right angle, your vulva opens up for him like a sweet, honey-dripping flower. Men want to know that their tremendous sexual prowess is propelling their partners to the heights of ecstasy. But never forget that, most of the time, they are completely mystified about what *really* turns women on. How provocatively refreshing it is, then, to be shown in such a nonthreatening and salaciously seductive way *exactly* how to drive you wild in bed!

Reason #5. You can learn hot new tricks from your man too. Not long after I vibrated my way to sexual self-rediscovery, I met Michael, a dedicated and natural sensualist. Sometimes I brought my vibrator to bed with us, but what Michael really wanted to see was me stroking myself between the legs, swelling, undulating, and oozing delicious, slippery moisture. He used to love watching me give myself an orgasm with my fingers and often said it was the most erotic thing he'd ever seen. I loved to watch him, too. In fact, that's how I learned most of what I know about exciting a man's penis. By watching him pleasure his own, I found out, for example, about that "one slow, five fast strokes" routine that drives most men insane.

Clearly, self-pleasuring with a partner can provide an electrifying boost to any couple's love life. But whether you discuss its lusty virtues with your mate beforehand—to feel him out, prepare, and excite him—or make it a sizzling surprise, it's probably best to start with a small, unintimidating sample of your self-pleasuring power. Over the next several days or lovemaking sessions, take your cues from each other, slowly getting used to your new erotic freedom, before you gradually crescendo to a stirring display of autoerotic fireworks. You'll probably both feel more comfortable that way.

194. Sometime during foreplay look him straight in the eye as you suck the tip of your forefinger and slide it seductively over your lips. Then use your wet fingertip to tease his lips and mouth or to give your nipples a slippery pinch, or insert it smoothly into your vagina. Although his eyes will be riveted to your actions, keep him physically involved too by using your other hand to massage his body somewhere.

195. As a variation on number 194, start by brazenly wetting your finger in *his* mouth before trailing it over, under, and into your body.

196. Cup your breasts in your hands and present them to him. Bring your nipples to his mouth, lift his hand

to them, or play provocatively with them yourself. Deliberately twirl, tweak, pull, and pinch in the ways that make you hot, so he'll learn something while he's getting an erection.

197. Provocatively slather oil on your breasts and then take your pleasure on his body, rubbing your slick, tingly nipples roughly or gently all over his face, neck, chest, nipples, stomach, legs, buns, testicles, and penis. Slide his toes, knees, flattened hand, and finally his hardened penis between your pearly globes. Let your deeply satisfied moans inflame him even further.

198. As a variation on the previous suggestion, do the same with your oiled pubic hair and vulva or (a personal favorite of my lover's) with your well-lubricated bottom.

199. Give your man a tactile and sensual thrill by asking him to lick your fingers while you massage your hottest erogenous zones.

200. Take photos of yourself massaging your body and send them to him, insert them in the folds of his newspaper, or leave them propped up on his pillow.

201. Some women prefer to blindfold themselves when first self-pleasuring for their lovers. Says my shy

friend Milly, "I can be in my own private world and feel free to do all sorts of naughty things I'd be too embarrassed to do otherwise. Sometimes I even keep the blindfold on after we start making love because the feeling of not knowing what's coming next and the heightened sense of touch are so exciting." In fact, not being under the scrutiny of your gaze can be freeing for your partner too.

202. You might try supplementing what your man is doing to you with *his* hands. A sensuous publishing exec I know says, "When my husband has his fingers in my vagina, it feels more intimate if I stroke his hand with mine. Sometimes I rub my clitoris or massage my outer lips against his fingers. We have fun getting our fingers all tangled up together."

203. Another opportunity for partial privacy is when your lips are locked together in a passionate kiss and your eyes are closed or busy staring into each other's orbs. This is a good time to stroke his back with one hand and massage your breasts or vulva with the other. He just makes you so *hot!*

204. Incorporate any of the sense-awakening activities from Chapter 2 into your partner self-pleasuring. Take a bath with him and run the water and your soapy

hands over your genitals and his. Dance for him while seductively undulating your hands over your private places. Use flowers, feathers, or fur to stroke yourself, and him, provocatively. Pour wine over your breasts or genitals, rub it in, lick your fingers, and press your wine-soaked parts against him. Smooth ice over your nipples and into the narrow glove of your sex, then let him lick off the cold drippings.

205. One closet vamp I know likes to use her lover's body as a self-stimulating tool. She says, "I rub my vulva against his knee, foot, or fanny cheeks. Or I tickle my breast with his chest hairs or pinch a nipple between his toes. Sometimes I insert his big toe in my vagina and use it like a dildo. Of course I'm fingering my clit the whole time, too, and looking him straight in the eye."

206. Actually, one of the best self-pleasuring toys you'll ever have is your man's very own love rod. Use it, slippery with your lubrication but firmly ensconced in your caressing hand, to trace circles around your clitoris; to tease your inner lips and coral opening; to tickle your nipples; to massage your facial muscles; and, keeping it decidedly under the control of your maddening grasp, to inflame the inner walls of your vagina.

207. Several sex toys have been specifically designed to transform your lover's penis into an even more exciting self-pleasuring tool for you. The fact that you show up with one of them in the bedroom will ignite his lustful imagination even before you start. Latex or rubber rings with beads in them or soft prongs all around can be slipped down to the base of your man's organ. The snug fit increases his erection, and the beads or prongs rub deliciously against your vaginal lips and clitoris as he thrusts in and out of you. The beaded ones can also be made smaller to fit around the base of his penis head, thus providing you with an outrageous internal massage. French ticklers, or rubber sleeves that fit over the penis and sport nubs all over or feathery plumes on the end, also tease your insides and may quickly stimulate you into a frenzied vaginal orgasm. How potent he'll feel then!

208. My friend Liana's husband loves to watch her do the vacuuming while she's dressed in her leather corset or lace teddy. To further relieve the boredom of this mundane task, Liana occasionally reaches down to massage her exposed love nest. And of course it just so happens that she has to bend over then to examine a speck of dust on the carpet, giving her husband a spectacular view. Apparently she sometimes rubs the humming vacuum cleaner wand between her thighs, too. I always wondered how she got her husband to help with the housework!

209. Men love to see a woman spread her sex lips wide while she plays with herself, but women often feel hesitant to do this because they think it must look grotesque. On the contrary, men find the sight intensely erotic and beautiful. One lover of mine watched fascinated as he moaned over and over, "You're so pretty, so pretty. Yes, open that flower for me." Soon he simply had to join in.

210. My friend Teresa, who's been ecstatically married to the same man for thirty years, says she likes to cup, lift, and massage her fanny while her man is on top during intercourse. In addition to providing a deeper angle of entry, this adds rear stimulation that excites her immensely. And when she wants to come, she can easily slip her finger into her anus and start the spasms rolling.

211. When he is taking you from behind, massage your breasts or reach down to rub your love bud. Again, you may want to include him in the massage by occasionally stroking his thrusting penis while you're in the neighborhood.

212. You can, of course, pleasure yourself from any lovemaking position, but spoon fashion is a particularly good one because your hands and the front of your body are completely free and, as you don't face each other, any embarrassment can easily be hidden. Even the mys-

tery of what your man can't see you doing but can feel in your undulating response is a veiled enticement for him. Anyway, most men are very aroused when a woman gets so excited, presumably by him, that she just has to touch herself erotically. So if you have any doubts, you may want to try the spoon position as a seductive starter.

213. Speaking of lovemaking positions, when you are lying on your stomach and he's taking you from behind, use the friction of the sheet or pillow to graze against your nipples and clitoris. Your deepened undulations will turn up the heat in his body as well as yours.

214. Sometimes it's easier to abandon your inhibitions when you dress up like a tart. As a birthday present for my man, I once donned a red lace merry widow with garters and stockings (no panties!) and let him ogle me as I stood up on the bed to dance, wriggle, and seductively stroke all my exposed parts. Later he raved that it was the best birthday present he ever received.

215. Tie him up and make him watch you give yourself an orgasm. Concentrate on your arousal, letting him see just what kind of stroking, pressure, speed, and positions best turn you on. When you've had your first climax, untie him and allow him to join in the fun of bringing you to another.

216. Occasionally remove your wet finger from your glistening, musky depths and put it in his mouth to suck.

217. A bank teller I know says, "My lover gets wildly excited when I kneel over his chest, pinning down his arms with my legs, and then rub my clit and vagina. He says he loves to see my aroused sex and the ecstasy on my face, feel my tensed muscles, hear my panting, and inhale my scent. He usually has just enough arm movement to stroke his penis and time his orgasm with mine."

218. When you are on top during intercourse, give him an additional show and yourself greater pleasure by sitting up straight and massaging your flushed breasts. You may want to occasionally wet your finger in your mouth or vagina and moisten your stiffened nipple with it. Or lean back and stroke your clitoris as you keep thrusting on him.

219. When you feel especially bold, try kneeling over his face as you stroke your vaginal lips. He'll love the view; and you can occasionally allow him to lick you.

220. One bawdy friend of mine shares the following: "Nothing makes my boyfriend hotter than when I stroke his shaft to get him hard and start his pre-ejaculate fluids going. I take some on my fingers and put it in my mouth or massage my nipples or clit with it. Another thing I love to do is rub myself all over with his come juice. It's a great lubricant for self-massage, and it drives him crazy to watch me do this."

221. Self-pleasuring is a lovely accompaniment to oral sex as well. When he has his tongue buried in your dewy depths, you can get so carried away that you abandon restraint to massage your clitoris or caress your thighs and breasts. Or you can get the urge as you're kissing him too. As one very ladylike matron told me, "I feel so primal when I lick my husband's penis that a different me comes out. I don't feel shy at all about rubbing myself at the same time and even imitating with my fingers what I'd like him to be doing inside me. I always give him a good view of this, too, because it makes him really excited."

222. When you have both become more comfortable with this type of love-play, you should encourage your man to pleasure himself for you as well. It's highly erotic to watch each other simultaneously and to respond, even from a small distance, to the other's building arousal and orgasm. You can lie next to or opposite each other, legs perhaps entwined, and feast your eyes and senses for hours—or you can get a little more aggressive about it. One new bride, who was obviously getting her marriage

off to a flaming start, told me, "I'll never forget the excitement of watching my lover, kneeling between my outspread legs as I masturbated for him, stroking his engorged penis to orgasm right above me. Neither one of us could take our eyes off the spectacle of the other's sex in full, pulsing bloom. It was magnificent!" When you do this, try to retain some shred of your rational mind to observe how he is specially treating his love organ—that way, you'll know just how to make it your own later.

223. Self-pleasuring with your lover by phone can also be quite titillating. My friend Sara, who carried on a long-distance romance for over a year, says, "I used to talk to Jeff with one hand on the receiver and the other between my legs. I'd give him a blow-by-blow description of what I was doing, panting and moaning into the phone, or even putting the mouthpiece down below so he could hear the wet sounds I was making. Sometimes I'd start masturbating first and then call his answering machine as I got excited enough to come—and there'd just be these long drawn-out 'Ooooooo's' for a sexy message. He never looked at another woman the whole time he was gone."

224. The best way to overcome any jealousy your man might feel about your vibrator or dildo is to bring it to bed with you and let him play too. Share with him the lusty creature you become when a vibrator is throbbing you to orgasm, and be sure to pet him a little at the same time. Then use your toy gently on him. Let him see how delicious it looks when you tease yourself with a dildo, telling him you always imagine it's his lovely thick limb, and invite him to thrust the dildo powerfully inside you while his own equipment is free to cradle elsewhere—like in your cleavage, the cleft of your bottom, or between your buttery love lips. Or put on sexy lingerie and give him his own personal X-rated show, with you as the female lead gyrating in flagrant abandon with the male star—your vibrating dildo. If you always involve him and let him see more of your passion than he'd normally be privileged to view, your toys will become not a threat but favorite tools for joint self-pleasures.

225. My friend Catherine has a very clever suggestion for including your man in the vibrator action. She says that when her husband is making love to her from behind, she often presses a vibrator to her thighs, pelvic mound, or clitoris. Not only does this raise her passion to fever heat, but it also transmits tingling pulsations to her lucky fellow's erection right through the walls of her throbbing flesh. Or when they are face-to-face, she simply lodges a small battery-powered vibrating dildo between her genitals and his. That way, each time he thrusts, they both get a powerful quivering jolt.

226. Remember all those suggestions in Chapter 9 for using a vibrator on the back of your hand while your fingers tantalize your clitoris, vaginal walls, or G-spot? Well, simply substitute your lover's hand for your own, slipping his fingers seductively between the vibrator and your trembling flesh. He'll love participating firsthand in your pulsing, swelling excitement.

227. With or without a vibrator, you might drive your man wildest of all by bringing yourself to the frenzied peak just before orgasm while he watches in panting fascination, then stopping completely, looking at him with fever in your eyes, and moaning, "Come fuck me *now!*"

She learned to be at home
in her body, to be her
own best friend, her
favourite lover.

—*Tee Corrinne,*

<u>Dreams of the Woman</u>

<u>Who Loved Sex</u>

/ /
---
daily
goddess-
izers

"I make time for self-pleasuring every day, even if I have to lock myself in the bathroom, skip lunch, or tell my mate to give me an hour by myself. If I didn't, I'd be stressed out at work, a boring lover, and a crabby witch to my friends and family. They deserve better than that, and so do I."

—Anne, executive secretary

"My sexuality makes me feel alive, important, and good about myself."

—Sandy, housewife and mother of six children

"It makes me feel great to know that we women can be many different kinds of people, professional as well as sexy."

—Jennifer, computer specialist

"The more time I spend getting in touch with my inner sensuality, the better my day seems to go. It gets my sex hormones flying, and then men are drawn to me like magnets."

—Lelia, retired attorney

like riding a bicycle, the knack of unleashing your auto-erotic Sex Goddess is not lost if you don't do it all the time.

But I've found that the greatest benefits of keeping her active in your life—enhanced health, well-being, and energy; stress reduction; charismatic self-confidence; hot lovemaking expertise; and constant sexual radiance—are made fully available only if you keep your self-pleasuring thermostat on high with regular practice. Smart, sexy women, like the ones quoted above, pleasure themselves and their Inner Sex Goddess—even if only in some small, five-minute way—every single day. Besides innately understanding that self-pleasure is necessary for their physical, emotional, and mental well-being, they feel it's a precious and delightful gift they love to unwrap as often as possible.

Like them, you should bestow upon yourself the same love and attention you would naturally give any romantic relationship. That's what keeps love affairs (and lovers) healthy, hot, and juicy. A love affair with yourself is no different. So schedule time for sensuality; delegate household chores to children, mate, or cleaning person; give up an hour at the health club; skip part of a gossip session (giving up gossip completely is of course unthinkable); knock a half hour off your shopping; do whatever you have to do to establish your self-pleasuring as a priority. Never forget that you *deserve* to live in a perpetually fresh garden of ecstatic delights. And, as a reigning Sex Goddess, your glorious kingdom extends to those you love and care for.

daily goddessizers

Even if you are the busiest woman on the planet, I'm sure you can find time for at least one of these quick and easy goddessizers every day. They'll keep your sensual motor purring and your Inner Sex Goddess glowing.

- In your morning shower, let the water run over your beautiful genitals. As you wash, massage your clitoris and dip your soapy fingers into your vagina.
- As you towel off, rub the rough terry cloth against your soft vulva.
- When you apply body lotion, massage your nipples for an extra minute.
- Admire your naked body as you dress. Preen, pose, and play.
- Whenever you go to the bathroom, touch your vulva lovingly.
- Move through your whole day being turned on by sounds, smells, beautiful scenes, awareness of your sexual juices, the sight of someone's full mouth, provocative ads, a glimpse of the moon.
- Caress a tree on the way to work.
- Sensitize your clitoris by lightly stroking it for ten minutes every day.

- Roll in fur.
- Squeeze and rub your thighs together, especially when you're on the gym machines.
- Exercise naked.
- Flex your PC muscle whenever you think of it; no one at the meeting will know.
- Stand in the wind, close your eyes, open your palms, inhale its freshness.
- Flash yourself in the mirror.
- Invent a hot fantasy while riding the bus to work, standing in line at the bank, or under the hair dryer at the beauty salon.
- Choose your lunch menu based on color and fragrance. Admire, lick, and smell your food.
- Give your Inner Sex Goddess a mental hug at least once every day. Like you, she thrives on attention, love, and praise. Ask her advice on what to wear.
- Indulge in a chocolate-covered ice-cream bar. Rub it on your lips and anywhere else you can get away with.
- Whenever you look in a mirror, tell yourself, "I love you. You are intelligent, powerful, sexy, beautiful, and irresistible." Blow yourself a kiss if no one's looking.
- While talking on the phone, massage your face, neck, and breasts.
- Occasionally bring your attention to your *hara*

(located about two inches below your navel), considered by martial arts specialists to be the body's center of gravity and power. This snaps you immediately into the present moment and the world of the senses. Float there as you experience your own sensuality, remaining motionless or stroking yourself luxuriously.

• Dance the hula as you file or dust.

• Self-pleasure in the "exotic" locations you visit every day—the ladies' room at work, a telephone booth, a restaurant bathroom stall, someone else's backyard, or an empty meeting room.

• On the commuter train, feel the heavy vibrations come up through your feet and into your legs, thighs, and pelvis. Let your body hum.

• Punctuate your housecleaning with short vibrator sessions—ten minutes fully clothed on the couch with the vibrator, ten minutes vacuuming, ten minutes back on the couch, ten minutes dusting, and so on.

• Wash dishes in the nude.

• Doodle pictures of body parts and other sensuous things. Write in your journal about all of the erotic things you've seen, smelled, touched, heard, and done today.

• In the grocery store, fondle the cucumbers and zucchini.

• Treat your self-pleasuring as a brief meditation. Close your eyes and drift in the alpha brain waves produced by using a vibrator on your erogenous zones. Tune in to your sensual intuition, daydreams, and creative juices.

• Lying in bed at night, massage and love your body. Go to sleep thinking of yourself as a sensual wonderland, a famous temptress, or the answer to your man's erotic dreams.

for special, languorous occasions

When you do have time for a longer, more luxurious visit with your Inner Sex Goddess, treat yourself to:

• an hour-long hot scented bath with candles, music, and wine
• an extended version of any of the "Seeds of Sensuality" activities from Chapter 2
• the hottest and longest fantasy or role-play you can dream up, complete with toys, clothes, and props
• the ritual of the Mirror of Sensual Transformation, with or without a vibrator
• a two-hour teasing session in which you bring yourself to the peak at least fifteen times before

you finally allow yourself to explode into one earth-shattering orgasm

- a two-hour teasing session in which you give yourself fifteen orgasms
- an X-rated video accompanied by candles, incense, wine, and a vibrator
- a lazy afternoon with a fantasy or real life love slave
- a languorous self-massage with aromatherapy oils or in a hot bath
- two hours of reading or writing erotic literature, massaging your breasts and genitals the whole time

For an extra treat, try this lovely Tantric sensual meditation:

Stimulate yourself to a peak of excitement, then close your eyes and focus on your *relaxed* breathing. Imagine yourself to be *in* your perineum or clitoris. Feel a sensation, heat, tingle, shape, color, or sound there. As you continue pleasuring yourself, breathe energy into this area and let your special sensation expand as you exhale. After a few moments move your imagined location high up into your womb and feel a different sensation there. Repeat the breathing and expanding. Next, travel to your navel with the same process, and then to your heart. As you fully experience the warmth and love in your heart, finally let yourself have an orgasm that washes deliciously over your entire body. Bask for a while in your sensual Nirvana before reentering the everyday world.

Your Inner Sex Goddess brings pleasure, confidence, and joy not only to you but, through you, to all those in your life. A whole world of women in such full sensual flower would be a beautiful garden indeed. So, like all of the mythological and real-life sex goddesses you've read about in this book, don't be afraid to get really decadent and outrageous. On the contrary, be proud of your multifaceted, lusty creativity. Remind yourself every day that you are a luscious, highly erotic woman—a true Sex Goddess divinely designed for pleasure and loving.

Freely radiate your resplendent sensuality, and the whole world will be transformed into your divine kingdom of love.

Appendix

the inner sex goddess scrolls

books, magazines, music, and videos to get you in the mood

Of the millions of erotic books, magazines, videos, and pieces of music out there, here are just a few that have been highly recommended by the Inner Sex Goddesses of many ultra-sensual women (including my own) especially for self-arousal. Try them out and see which ones resonate for you. If you find a particular work that really brings your Aphrodite self out to play, explore the other pieces that author, composer, or director has done too. Visit your local sex toy store or browse the pages of home pleasure toy catalog or adult magazines for further choices. Shop the erotica section of your favorite bookstore. Ask the clerk at the video or music store for recommendations. Share suggestions with your friends. Keep your eyes and ears open and your Inner Sex Goddess antennae alert; once you start looking, you'll find that all sorts of wonderful erotica shows up naturally within your Sensual Domain. Happy trolling!

Literature

Delta of Venus by Anaïs Nin (actually *anything* by Nin is fabulously erotic)

Fanny Hill by John Cleland

Lady Chatterley's Lover and *Women in Love* by D. H. Lawrence

Cheri by Colette

Emmanuelle by Emmanuelle Arsan

The Story of O by Pauline Reáge

The Pearl by a collection of Victorian authors

Plaisir d'Amour by Anne-Marie Villefranche

The Pleasures of Loving, compiled by Maren Sell

The Black Cat books, any of them, published by Grove Press

Tropic of Cancer by Henry Miller

The Naked Lunch by William Burroughs

The Claiming of Sleeping Beauty, Beauty's Punishment, and *Beauty's Release* by A. N. Roquelaure

Exit to Eden by Anne Rice

The Erotic Comedies, or anything else, by Marco Vassi

The Gates of Paradise, edited by Alberto Manguel

Lust, edited by John and Kirsten Miller

My Secret Garden and *Forbidden Flowers* by Nancy Friday

Pleasures: Women Write Erotica by Lonnie Barbach, Ph.D.

Endless Love by Scott Spencer

The Intimate Kiss by Gershon Legman

"Song of Solomon" from the Bible

Erotic Poems, edited by Peter Washington

The Book of Eros, edited by Lily Pond and Richard Russo

Art Books

The Art of Arousal by Dr. Ruth Westheimer

The Erotic Edge by Lonnie Barbach, Ph.D.

The Erotic Arts by Peter Webb

Erotic Art of the East and *Primitive Erotic Art* by Philip Rowson

Adult Magazines

Playgirl

Woman on Top

Playboy

Penthouse (great for the pictorials with people making love)

Penthouse Letters (*hot* letters from readers)

Yellow Silk (collections of erotic writing)

Tantra

For Women

Paramour

Classical Music

Hungarian Rhapsody #2 by Liszt

Bolero by Ravel

The 1812 Overture by Tchaikovsky

Scheherazade by Rimsky-Korsakov

Symphony No. 9 ("Ode to Joy") by Beethoven

Canon in D Major by Pachelbel

Romeo and Juliet by Prokofiev

Meditation by Mischa Maisky, cello

The Double Life of Veronique soundtrack by Krzysztof Kies-
lowsky

Carmina Burana by Orff

The Firebird by Stravinsky

Suite No. 3 in D Major by Bach

"Love Death" aria from *Tristan und Isolde* by Wagner

"Celeste Aida" from *Aida* by Verdi

"O soave fanciulla" from *La Bohème* by Puccini

"Tu, tu, amore tu?" from *Manon Lescaut* by Puccini

Carmen by Bizet

Modern Music

"Leila" (original or "unplugged" version) by Eric Clapton

"Brown Sugar," "Let's Spend the Night Together," or
countless other hits by the Rolling Stones

"Fields of Gold" by Sting

"Lay, Lady, Lay" by Bob Dylan

"Knights in White Satin" by the Moody Blues

"Black Magic Woman" by Santana

"Baby, Baby" by Smokey Robinson

"Let Me Stand Next to Your Fire" by Jimi Hendrix

"Stir It Up" by Bob Marley

"Love Me Tender" by Elvis Presley

Inside the Taj Mahal (flute) by Paul Horn

"Dream Lover" by Mariah Carey

"Crazy for You" by Madonna

"Caribbean Queen" by Billy Ocean

Rhythm of the Saints by Paul Simon

"You Make Me Feel Like a Natural Woman" by Aretha Franklin

"Fly Me to the Moon" by Frank Sinatra

"Unforgettable" by Natalie and Nat King Cole

"Sweetest Taboo" by Sade

CrazySexyCool by TLC

"Purple Rain" by Prince

"Sex" by Morphine

"Funky Blues" by Charlie Parker

"Fooled Around and Fell in Love" by Elvin Bishop

Taj Mahal by Taj Mahal

Compact Jazz by Antonio Carlos Jobim

Nouveau Flamenco by Ottmar Liebert

Dreams by Kitaro

Enigma by Enigma

Chariots of Fire soundtrack by Vangelis

Adult Videos

Behind the Green Door
Delta of Venus
The Seven Seductions
Pandora's Mirror
Taboo American Style

Night Trips, House of Dreams, Hidden Obsessions (and *any* other films directed by Andrew Blake—he's one of the best)

Three Daughters (and any other films put out by Candida Royale and her Femme Productions; they are specifically directed toward women)

The Licorice Quartet (and anything else directed by Harry Paris)

Boiling Point, Cat House, The Girl with the Heart-Shaped Tattoo (and any other films directed by Toni English, a woman)

Better Sex (an instructional series)

Red Shoe Diaries (the half-hour TV series from Showtime)